Karen Wallace lives in Herefordshire with her husband and two children. Her previous books include *The Pan Picnic Guide* (1983)

HEREFORDSHIRE FOOD

KAREN WALLACE

ARCH

ISBN 0-94761-802-3

CIP data:

Wallace, Karen
Herefordshire Food : new and traditional recipes from the county's best kitchens.
1. Cookery, English
I. Title
641.59424'4 TX717

Published by ARCH,Lower Grantsfield,
Kimbolton, Leominster, Herefordshire HR6 OET

Cover illustration: *The Hop Pickers* (1858) by T. J. Banks, reproduced by kind permission of the Lower Nupend Gallery and Oscar and Peter Johnson Ltd.

Printed and bound in Great Britain
by Billings & Sons Limited, Worcester.

Contents

Introduction	7
Starters	11
Fish	23
Poultry and Game	33
Meat	43
Light lunches and Suppers	53
Puddings	57
Cakes	73
Drinks, Pickles and Preserves	83

Introduction

Herefordshire people are surrounded on all sides by food. The county is famous for its lamb, beef and game, while its dairy herds produce the raw material for cheese, custards, curds and yoghurts. The county's rivers produce salmon, pike, grayling and trout, and in the late summer some of England's most famous orchards are loaded with apples, pears, and plums. But amazingly enough, there has never until now been a book written about Herefordshire Food.

When I began assembling this book, it seemed at first that Herefordshire people of bygone days were too busy getting on with their lives to worry much about what might be on their plates at mealtimes. Then I discovered a book of recipes, beautifully handwritten by Elizabeth Foley in 1693, and slowly a food map of the county began to emerge. There was a recipe for " Crawfish Soop " (*sic*) - crayfish were once plentiful in Herefordshire rivers, and can still be found in some. There were many suggestions for cooking pigeons; the dovecotes that are one of Herefordshire's architectural glories were once a major source of food. There were ways of preserving and cooking beef and lamb from the farms. And the richness of Elizabeth Foley's puddings testifies not only to the availability of fruit, but to the abundance of milk and eggs. Her recipe for " A Sack Possett " begins: " Take fourteen eggs leave out half y^{r} whites... [and a] quart of cream boyling hott".

Elizabeth Foley's book reads as much like a social history as a collection of recipes. Like all the household books of the time, it contains local remedies and superstitions. For example, after instructions on how to make a pippin tansy comes " an excellent thing to bring a man to life when he is fallen into a fitt of appiplexey." The remedy was to fry a bag of salt and place it, still hot, on the stomach of the sufferer. She goes on to add: "a man was brought to life this way that had been dead for 2 days".

I was surprised at the sophistication of some of her recipes and I have included my favourite one in the fish section. It is a recipe for baking pike " my mother's way " - so it must be one of the oldest recipes in the book. The fish is stuffed, wrapped in layer after layer of wilted spinach, and sealed with egg, the whole acting as a sort of seventeenth-century tinfoil. The result is a marvellously moist fish, with the bonus that you can eat the wrapping as well.

Almost one hundred years later, Anne Ward of Gatley Park sat down and wrote her own cookery book. There is something sedate and sensible about this collection, as befits the eighteenth century - the Age of Reason. Again the collection includes contemporary medicines and cures, but the superstition and magic of Elizabeth Foley's day has gone. Anne Ward was a practical woman, skilled in the art of household management. After a recipe for Raspberry Cakes, she gives the ingredients for a " cheap paint for Gates and Rails," using (among other things) two quarts of skim milk.

Many recipes sent to me in the course of my research for this book came accompanied by stories. One intriguing tale came from Thomas Jay of Canon Pyon, who told me that when his great- grandparents moved to a house called The Highway at Lyde, they kept a bench stocked with bread, cheese and cider to feed the wandering bands of vagrant soldiers left over from the Napoleonic Wars. The bench has gone now, but the cubbyhole through which the victuals were passed can still be seen.

The many country houses of Herefordshire have their own culinary legacy. One of them, Garnons, to the west of Hereford, has been the seat of the Cotterell family for almost two hundred years. The present Lady Cotterell introduced me to Mrs. Iris Jones, who worked in the kitchens there for some twenty-six years. Mrs. Jones began as a kitchen maid and eventually became the cook for the household. She is retired now, and I have tried to include with her recipes some of her delightful stories of life beyond the green baize door. She loved cooking, and especially enjoyed decorating and presenting dishes for dinner parties. In those days the job of cook was a very busy one. Apart from the three main meals of the day, there was tea with sandwiches and cakes and a whole range of pickling and preserving to be done. They even roasted their own coffee, using beans sent up by rail from the Army & Navy Stores in London. Dinner was a six-course meal, and the sheer amount of food prepared was amazing. Mrs. Jones writes in her diary: "how they ate all that much I do not know...I expect they only had an eyeful of each course." Doubtless a tribute to her presentation!

In choosing the recipes for this book I have tried not only to combine old and new but wherever possible to tell the story of each recipe as it appears. There are many good cooks in Herefordshire today whose recipes may well become "traditional" in time. I have consulted a number of them, both professional and amateur.

Patricia Hegarty's family has lived in Herefordshire for 700 years. Her interest in food stems from the late 1970s, when she and her husband John turned their present home at Hope End, near Ledbury, into a small hotel. Hope End was the childhood home of Elizabeth Barrett Browning. It has an acre of walled garden, containing some forty different vegetables and a large informal herb bed. Patricia believes that close links should exist between kitchen, garden and countryside, so her cooking style combines the excellence of local ingredients with a keen enthusiasm for the tastes and techniques of earlier periods in English cooking. Patricia was enormously helpful in testing recipes for me, and I have also included a number of her own dishes straight from the kitchen at Hope End.

Effy's Restaurant started in Hay-on-Wye in 1979. It was the combined talents of Elly Parker, Helen Powers, and Neffy Hensher which put the restaurant into *The Good Food Guide* a few months later. Like Patricia Hegarty, they use local ingredients - including lamb and vegetables from the Parkers' own farm in Vowchurch. Their style of cooking is hard to pin down; they take the best from various schools, but also create wonderfully original dishes like the Blackberry and Apple

Mousse Tart included in this book. In 1983 Effy's moved to Hereford, and in 1985 it became the first restaurant in the city to gain an entry in *The Michelin Guide*.

Many other people have helped me in preparing this book. I should like to thank Ivor and Susie Dunkerton of Dunkerton's Cider, Mark Capper of Stocks Vineyards (who produces an excellent white wine from vineyards on the Herefordshire/ Worcestershire borders), Jenny Allday of Country Cooks, Ros Fry, Suzanne Davies at the Museum of Cider, Olive Odell, Eric Lindsey-Jones, Gus Woodward, Ann Searle, Andrew Foley for his kind permission to use the Elizabeth Foley book, and Thomas Dunne for his permission to use Anne Ward's cookery book. Finally, very special thanks must go to Sue Hubbard and her staff at the Hereford Records Office, where I spent many hours poring over books and papers and taking great advantage of their knowledge and helpfulness.

Starters

Cider Garlic Bread

Serves 4

Ivor and Susie Dunkerton have their own cider press just outside Pembridge. Since cider is so much a part of their lives, it is not surprising that it should have found its way into their kitchen as well.

1 loaf of crusty French bread
3 oz (75 g) melted butter
3 cloves garlic crushed
1 tablespoon (1x15 ml spoon) finely chopped parsley or chervil
8 oz (225 g) grated cheese
1/4 pint (150 ml) dry cider

Cut the bread lengthwise, but not quite through. Mix the butter, garlic, parsley and cheese. Put the bread on a large piece of tinfoil. Spread the butter mixture over the inside of the bread. Pour over the cider, which the bread will soak up. Wrap the foil closely round the loaf and put in an oven at 350°, Gas Mark 4, for 30 minutes. Open up the foil while the bread is still cooking and bake for a further five minutes so it becomes crusty.

Sorrel Soup

Serves 6

This is a refreshing soup with a sharp lemony taste from Patricia Hegarty, who owns the Hope End Country House Hotel in Ledbury. If you live on the acid soils of west Herefordshire, you will probably find sorrel growing wild in the meadows.

1 medium onion
1 medium potato
1 oz (25 g) butter
2 pints (1.2 litres) chicken stock
18 medium-sized sorrel leaves
sea salt
pepper

Wash the sorrel leaves and tear out the central spine. Chop the onion and slice the potato. Melt the butter in a saucepan and soften the onion. Add the potato and cook for a few minutes. Add the sorrel leaves and cook until the sorrel 'melts'. Finally pour in the chicken stock and cook gently until the potato is soft. Put the soup in a blender and process until smooth. Strain and season. Serve immediately. Do not add cream to this soup, or it will curdle

Uncle Dick's Onion Soup

Serves 8

This unusual soup uses both honey and cider, and comes from Susie Dunkerton.

2 lbs (almost 1 kilo) large onions finely sliced 2 tablespoons (2 x l5 ml spoons) cooking oil
3 oz (75 g) butter
l tablespoon (l x l5 ml spoons) honey
3 tablespoons (3 x l5 ml spoons) flour
3/4 pint (450 ml) dry cider

4 pints (2.2 litres) stock or water
wineglass of red wine or port
salt and pepper
parsley

Melt the butter, oil and honey in a heavy saucepan. Add the onions and gently cook for half an hour until they are golden brown. Stir in the flour. Add the heated stock and cider. Simmer and stir to thicken. Season with salt and pepper and simmer for 40 minutes. Add wine or port. Let the soup stand for 5 minutes before serving sprinkled with parsley and croutons.

Cod and Mussel Soup

Serves 6 - 8

This delicious fish soup uses both cream and cider. It is well worth the time required to make it, and is a meal on its own with lots of hot garlic bread and a large salad.

20 mussels
1 wine bottle (3/4 litre) dry cider
1 teaspoon (1 x 5 ml spoon) thyme
2 medium-sized onions chopped
1 cod weighing 2-3 lbs (1 - 1.5 kilos)
1 leek chopped
2 stalks of celery chopped
1 bouquet garni
1/4 pint (150 ml) thick cream
3 oz (75 g) butter
salt and pepper
parsley
1 1/4 pints (750 ml) boiling water

Clean and scrape the mussels in running water, and pull off their beards. Put in a heavy pot with a lid over a high heat 1/4 pint (150 ml) cider, half the thyme and one chopped onion. Add the mussels and cover; cook for 6-8 minutes, shaking the pot occasionally so that all the mussels open. Let the liquid cool and remove the mussels from their shells. Put to one side.

Cut the head and tail off the fish. Skin and fillet it. Cut the fish into chunks and set aside. In a pot put the boiling water, 1 tablespoon (1 x 15 ml spoon) salt, the rest of the thyme and the skin and bones from the fish. Reduce this by half over a medium heat. Cool, strain and add this liquid to the mussel liquid. Put the rest of the cider in a pot and add the leeks, celery and onion, the bouquet garni, salt and pepper. Simmer for 30 minutes. Pass through a sieve or blend in a liquidizer. Mix with the fish and mussel stock. Add the cod chunks, the cream and butter. Simmer gently for 15 minutes. Finally add the mussels. Check the seasoning and sprinkle with parsley or chervil.

Gatley Park Turnip Soup

Serves 6

This recipe is adapted from Anne Ward's cookery book of 1789. It may be eaten hot, decorated with cream and a sprinkling of chives or it is equally good served very cold. Herefordshire's own vichyssoise!

1 lb (450 g) turnips
2 pints (1.1 litres) chicken stock, preferably homemade
1 carrot
1 small onion
1 teaspoon (1 x 5 ml spoon) salt
1 teaspoon (1 x 5 ml spoon) basil
1 teaspoon (1 x 5 ml spoon) marjoram
2 tablespoons (2 x 15 ml spoons) cream
good pinch cayenne pepper
cream and chives to decorate

Peel and chop the vegetables. Add them to the strained chicken stock and put in the herbs and salt. Do not add the pepper at this stage. Cook gently until the vegetables are soft. When cooked, remove the vegetables with a slotted spoon and put to one side. Strain the soup. Return the cooked vegetables to the liquid. Put in the blender or rub through a sieve until smooth. Add the cream and return to the saucepan if the soup is to be eaten hot. Season to taste with the pepper and add salt if necessary. Do not boil. Decorate with cream and chives.

If the soup is to be eaten cold, allow it to cool completely and refrigerate until well-chilled, then decorate with cream and chives.

Elizabeth Foley's Pea Soup

Serves 6

I found this recipe in a cookery book dated 1693. The original recipe calls for red herrings - one of the earliest forms of preserved fish, dating back to the Norman Conquest. At that time herrings were first salted and then smoked. They were then allowed to dry and smoked again and again. The end result was a dried-up red fish which could withstand time and travel and provided the staple food during periods of fasting such as Lent.

Red herrings had to be soaked for two or three hours in water or milk before they could be eaten, and even then they would have been extremely salty. Nowadays we have kippers, which are very lightly salted and smoked by comparison.

8 oz (225 g) dried split green peas
2½ pints (1.5 litres) water
1 onion stuck with 2 cloves
1 carrot
1 teaspoon (1 x 5 ml spoon) marjoram
1 teaspoon (1 x 5 ml spoon) basil
1 kipper, boned
3 anchovies
salt and pepper
1 oz (25 g) butter
3 tablespoons (3 x 15 ml spoon) single cream

Put the water, peas, onion, carrot and herbs into a saucepan. Do not add salt. Boil slowly for one hour. Remove the carrot and onion. Add the kipper and the anchovies cut into small pieces.

Simmer for 15 minutes.

Pour soup into a blender or rub through a sieve until smooth. Add the cream and the butter and blend thoroughly. Season to taste with salt and pepper. Serve with croutons and a little dried mint.

Almond Soup

Serves 8

The almond has a long and varied history both in the kitchens and the medicine cupboards of the county. Elizabeth Foley used it as a sort of seventeenth-century milk of magnesia, as well as the prime ingredient in a number of cakes and puddings. Here is Anne Ward's recipe for a delicious creamy white soup. In the original she suggests pouring the soup over a number of small French rolls stuck with split almonds in the bottom of a large tureen. I prefer croutons and a handful of almonds fried in butter.

For the stock:

2 lbs (almost 1 kilo) meaty veal bones or 1 chicken carcase
1 turnip
salt
blade of mace
water to cover

For the soup:

3 oz (70 g) ground almonds
1/2 pint (300 ml) milk
1/4 pint (150 ml) single cream
salt and cayenne pepper

Make the stock and simmer gently until it is reduced to 3 pints - 1.5 litres . Strain. Simmer the stock, almonds and milk together for twenty-five minutes. Put the mixture in a liquidizer and process for a few minutes. Return the soup to the heat and stir in the cream. Do not allow to boil. Serve immediately, sprinkled with croutons and split almonds fried in butter.

Potted Mushrooms

Serves 6

This recipe comes from Anne Ward's cookery book. The use of mace and cloves gives the mushrooms a distinctly old-fashioned flavour.

1 lb (450 g) small mushrooms
1/2 teaspoon (1 x 2.5 ml spoon) salt
good pinch ground mace
good pinch ground cloves
6 1/2 oz (165 g) butter

Wash and dry the mushrooms. Melt half the butter in a saucepan, put in the salt, mace and cloves, then add the mushrooms. Let them wilt over a very gentle heat for about fifteen minutes. Increase the heat slightly until half the liquid has boiled away. Then add the remaining butter and let them stew until all the liquid is gone and only the melted butter remains. Put the mushrooms into a pot, and press down lightly. If the butter does not cover them completely, clarify a little more and pour it over the top. Chill for 24 hours and serve with hot toast or fresh bread.

Calamanco

Serves 6 - 8

Calamanco is the rather exotic name given by Anne Ward to a traditional combination of potted tongue and chicken, spread in layers in a terrine, refrigerated, and then cut into slices.

The name comes from a glossy, striped wool cloth from Flanders, popular in the eighteenth century for the making of fancy waistcoats and breeches.

It is a most attractive first course, or can be included in a cold table. For best results, it should be prepared and refrigerated at least a day in advance.

8 oz (225 g) cooked chicken
1/2 teaspoon (1 x 2.5 ml spoon) ground nutmeg
1/2 teaspoon (1 x 2.5 ml spoon) ground mace
1 dessertspoon (1 x 10 ml spoon) lemon juice
4 oz (100 g) clarified butter
salt and pepper
8 oz (225 g) cooked pork or ox tongue
1/2 teaspoon (1 x 2.5 ml spoon) ground mace
4 oz (100 g) clarified butter
salt and pepper
2 oz (50 g) clarified butter

Pound together the chicken, nutmeg, mace, lemon juice, salt and pepper or put them all in a food processor and mix. Slowly add the clarified butter and continue mixing until the meat becomes a soft smooth paste. Repeat the process with the tongue, mace, salt and pepper. Spread the two mixtures in alternate layers in a small terrine. Seal with extra butter. Refrigerate for at least one day.

When it is to be served, take a sharp knife and cut around the meat. Turn out onto a plate and cut into slices. Arrange these on a serving dish and serve with brown toast.

Pheasant Terrine

Serves 8 - 10

This terrine comes from Lady Alexandra Cotterell, who lives at Garnons.It is a fine-looking dish and should be made at least one day in advance.

4 oz (100 g) pig's liver
8 oz (225 g) pork belly
8 oz (225 g) sausage meat
1 onion
1 clove garlic

8 oz (225 g) streaky bacon
1 pheasant (or any game bird)
1 bay leaf
a little consommé or jellied stock
salt and pepper

Grease a medium-sized terrine. Place a bay leaf in the middle and line the dish with streaky bacon. Mince the liver, belly pork and sausage meat - or ask the butcher to do it for you. Dice the onion, crush the garlic and add these to the mixture, with salt and pepper. Mix well. Put a layer of this at the bottom of the terrine. Cut thin slices from the pheasant and put these on top of the pork mixture. Alternate the two until the dish is full, preferably finishing with the pork mixture. Cover the dish as tightly as possible and place in a roasting pan half-filled with water. Cook for 1¼ hours in an oven pre-heated to 350°, Gas Mark 4.

When the terrine is cooked, remove it from the roasting pan and weight it down with a similar-sized tin loaded with two evenly spaced weights. Allow it to cool slightly, and pour in the warmed stock to fill the space around the sides of the dish. Refigerate for at least a day before serving.

Hare Pâté

Serves 8 - 10

This recipe comes from Mrs. Iris Jones, who worked at Garnons for twenty-six years, first as a kitchen maid and later as cook.

1½ lb (700 g) uncooked hare meat.
¼ lb (100 g) fat bacon
¾ lb (350 g) minced pork
1 egg
3 tablespoons (3 x 15 ml spoons) brandy
1 teaspoon (1 x 5 ml spoon) nutmeg
salt and pepper

Cut the hare into very small pieces and dice the bacon. Put this mixture into a bowl with the brandy and leave for two hours.

Mince the pork and then the hare and bacon mixture. Mix well and add the seasoning and egg. Press the whole mixture into a greased container, cover closely with foil and put in a roasting pan half-filled with water. Bake in a moderate oven, 350°, Gas Mark 4, for one hour. When cooked, remove from the roasting pan, weight (see Pheasant Terrine) and refrigerate overnight.

Ros Fry's Winter Salad

Serves 6

This salad may be eaten as a first course or a side salad. Jerusalem artichokes grow well in rich Herefordshire soil, and are often too prolific in a vegetable garden. They are a versatile and extremely nutritious vegetable. Ros maintains that careful peeling reduces their rather strident effect on the average digestive system.

¾ lb (350 g) Jerusalem artichokes
2 large carrots
1 large Cox apple
5 tablespoons (5 x 15 ml spoons) hazel or walnuts
juice of one lemon

The dressing is made from:

2 tablespoons (2 x 15 ml spoons) cider or wine vinegar
5 tablespoons (5 x 15 ml spoons) olive oil
(or 4 of olive oil and 1 of walnut oil)
½ teaspoon (1 x 2.5 ml spoon) salt
freshly ground pepper
chopped winter savoury, if available

Scrub the artichokes and steam them over plenty of boiling water for about 10 minutes, or until the skins come away easily. Remove the skins and return the roots to the steam to cook until they are just tender throughout. Set aside and allow to stand with the lid off while you make the dressing. Then slice them thinly into a bowl, and pour the dressing over them while they are still warm. Clean the carrots and peel the apple. Grate these into a bowl and mix with the juice of the lemon. Toast, skin and chop the nuts.

Take a deep glass dish and put a layer of the apple and carrot mixture in the bottom, then a layer of the artichokes in overlapping circles. Add a little extra dressing if they are not well coated, then a sprinkling of chopped nuts. Repeat this process until everything is used, finishing with the artichokes. Grind plenty of black pepper over the top and sprinkle with chopped nuts and any dressing left over. Let the salad stand in a cool place for at least an hour before serving.

Potted Trout

Serves 6 - 8

This is another of Anne Ward's recipes - typically eighteenth-century, but equally delicious in the 1980s. The original recipe calls for salmon but trout is more economical and just as good.

2 lbs (900 g) trout - three good fish
5 oz (125 g) butter
a good pinch each of ground mace, ginger, cloves and nutmeg
1 level teaspoon (1 x 5 ml spoon) salt
cayenne pepper
2 oz (50 g) clarified butter to seal

Skin and fillet the trout. Lightly grease a terrine and put a fillet of trout in the bottom, then some butter and a sprinkling of the mixed spices and seasoning. Repeat this layering until all the fish is used. Cover closely with foil and cook for 20 - 25 minutes at 350°, Gas Mark 4. When the fish is cooked, drain off the juices and lightly break up with a fork.

Skim off the butter from the fish juices and mix into the fish. Put the mixture into a serving dish and press down lightly. Clarify the remaining butter and pour carefully over the fish, Allow to cool completely and leave in the fridge overnight.

The fish is deliciously moist cooked in this way, and should be served with brown bread or toast.

Soft Roes with Lemon

Serves 4

Soft Roes were traditionally served at Garnons as a savoury course at the end of dinner, but they make an excellent starter sprinkled with freshly chopped parsley or chervil.

8 oz (225 g) soft herring roes
1½ oz (40 g) butter
1 lemon
seasoned flour
chopped parsley or chervil
salt and cayenne pepper

Roll the roes gently in seasoned flour. Melt the butter in a frying pan, and when it is foaming drop in the roes. Brown them on both sides, and sprinkle with a little salt and a pinch of cayenne pepper. Arrange them on hot buttered toast, decorate with parsley and serve with lemon quarters.

Fish

Cod or Pike Baked in Spinach

Serves 6

This recipe comes from Elizabeth Foley's cookery book, written in 1693. She says the cooking method comes from her mother, so the true date for this dish is much earlier. The original recipe calls for pike. I tried it with cod, and it was delicious. The fish looks particularly good in its spinach wrapping, which preserves the moisture and gives the skin a superb flavour.

1 cod or pike weighing 4 - 5 lbs (about 2 kilos)
5 oz (125 g) white breadcrumbs
6 anchovy fillets
good pinch nutmeg
2 teaspoons (2 x 5 ml spoons) basil
2 teaspoons (2 x 5 ml spoons) marjoram
1 oz (25 g) butter
2 eggs
about 20 spinach leaves
salt and pepper

Cut off the head and tail then clean and scale the fish. Rub it with salt and pepper. Melt the butter in a saucepan and mix in the breadcrumbs, nutmeg, herbs, salt, pepper, the anchovy fillets finely chopped, and the yolk of an egg. Make two gashes along the back of the fish. Fill these and the belly with the stuffing. Sew up the belly with strong cotton.

Break the remaining egg into a saucer and mix with the leftover white. Wash the spinach and break off the stalk of each leaf. Steam the leaves for two minutes or until they just wilt. Carefully wrap the leaves around the fish, smearing them with the raw egg mixture to hold them in place. There should be at least two complete layers of spinach leaves around the fish. With a pastry brush, paint the remaining egg mixture over the fish, which by now should look like a small green mummy. Tear three strips of tin foil and place them across a large roasting pan so that the edges hang over the sides. (These are to help remove the cooked fish onto the serving plate in one piece). Place the fish on top of the strips and bake in a cool oven at 275°, Gas Mark 1-2, for 1½ hours. Serve decorated with lemon slices and parsley.

Pickled Trout or Salmon

Serves 6

Pickled salmon was once very popular with Herefordshire gourmets. In the eighteenth century, Thomas Jones of Croft Castle sent barrels of the fish to various influential friends, in the hope of furthering his parliamentary ambitions.

There is also an account of a visit to Hereford in 1808, by a James Ely. He dined at the Greyhound Inn and ate pickled salmon which he found "a very high treat".

The recipe given below will suit either salmon or trout. For a salmon the amount of pickle would have to increase proportionally, but the method would be the same. One trout would serve two people for a starter, or one each for a main course.

6 medium-sized trout
1 pint (600 ml) water
1 pint (600 ml) wine vinegar
a dozen bruised coriander seeds
2 bay leaves
2 onions
salt and pepper

Cut the heads and tails off the fish. Clean and bone them but do not scale them. Split the fish and press them flat, skin side down, and cut away any bony bits with a very sharp knife. Rinse carefully and pat dry with a clean cloth. Slice the onions very thinly and lay slices down the length of each fillet. Season with pepper. Roll up the fillets and fit them tightly into a small earthenware or china terrine - do not use a metal dish. Pour over the water and vinegar, add a couple of pinches of salt, the bay leaves, coriander seeds and a good grind of pepper. Sprinkle over any remaining onion slices. Cover with foil. Cook in a cool oven, 275°, Gas Mark 1 - 2, for forty - five minutes. Leave the fish in the pickle for at least twenty-four hours. Serve with brown bread and butter.

(Mackerel may be prepared in the same way, substituting a tablespoon of pickling spice for the coriander seeds.)

Mackerel with Gooseberry Sauce

Serves 6

Always make sure the mackerel is fresh and allow one fish, weighing about 1 lb, per person.

6 mackerel
6 oz (150 g) butter
parsley
juice of a lemon
pepper and salt
1 lb (450 g) unripe gooseberries, topped and tailed
1/2 pint (300 ml) water

Cut the heads off the mackerel, clean them and wipe dry. With a sharp knife deeply score the fish with three diagonal cuts on each side. Make maître d'hôtel butter by mixing the butter, parsley, lemon juice, black pepper and a tiny pinch of salt. Melt half of this, and brush over the fish. Brush again with butter, reduce the grill to medium heat, and cook, basting frequently, for seven minutes. Turn the fish over and repeat the process.

Make a sauce by boiling the gooseberries in water until they are soft and thick. Put through a blender or rub through a sieve to get a smooth purée. Serve the fish on a hot plate with pats of the remaining butter dotted on the cuts. Put the sauce in a separate bowl. The tangy sharpness of the gooseberry sauce goes particularly well with the slightly oily mackerel flesh.

Grilled Grayling

Serves 6

The grayling is a freshwater fish related to the trout. It is common in many rivers in Herefordshire, and tastes every bit as good as trout. Grayling is said to feed on water thyme, and smells deliciously of the herb when it is cut open. Grayling do not usually grow larger than eighteen inches, and are best cooked simply. Allow one fish per person.

6 good grayling
6 oz (150 g) butter
good bunch each of fresh finely chopped chervil, chives, tarragon and parsley
salt and pepper

Clean the fish and make two diagonal cuts to the bone on both sides. Mix the butter with the chopped herbs, salt and pepper. Smear half the butter on the fish and into the cuts. Allow the grill to become very hot and grill on one side for four minutes. Remove the fish. Carefully turn them and repeat the process on the other side. Pour the juices over the fish and serve immediately.

Grayling à la Meunière

Serves 6

6 good grayling
6 oz (15) g) butter
1 tablespoon (1 x 15 ml spoon) chopped parsley
juice of a lemon

Clean the fish, and fillet them if they are large. Melt half the butter in a heavy frying pan and lightly fry the fish on both sides - about four minutes each way. Remove the fish and keep warm on a hot serving plate. Add the rest of the butter to the frying pan. When it is foaming, pour in the lemon juice and the chopped parsley. Pour this mixture over the fish and serve immediately.

Pickled Herrings

Serves 6

Pickled herrings are mentioned in Elizabeth Foley's cookery book. They need no cooking, as the flesh is preserved through the action of the vinegar. Pickled herrings make a delicious first course, but also fit nicely into a cold supper. Allow one fish per person.

6 herrings
3 pickled gherkins, sliced
3 shallots, sliced
1 dessertspoon (1 x 10 ml spoon) capers, finely chopped
1 pint (600 ml) wine vinegar
2 shallots, finely chopped
2 tablespoons (2 x 15 ml spoons) salt
2 whole cloves
6 black peppercorns
1 large bayleaf
pinch cayenne pepper or a few drops of Tabasco
1 teaspoon (1 x 5 ml spoon) sugar

Clean and fillet the herrings. Do not scale them. Flatten them, skin side down, and cover each fillet with a mixture of the capers, shallots and chopped gherkins. Roll the fillets as tightly as possible and secure them with toothpicks. Pack them gently in a terrine or glass jar with a tight- fitting lid. Make a marinade from the remaining ingredients. Bring the marinade slowly to the boil, and allow to cool completely before pouring over the fish. Cover closely and leave in a cool place or in the refrigerator for at least four days before serving.

Eels

River eels are very common in Herefordshire. After June, you should be able to get them in a good fishmonger's or from a local fisherman.

In 1653 Izaak Walton wrote, in *The Compleat Angler*, "eels are bred of a particular dew, falling in the months of May or June on the banks of some particular ponds or rivers, adapted by nature for that end; which in a few days are, by the sun's heat, turned into Eels." Nowadays, we know that eels come all the way from the Sargasso Sea.

Eel meat is delicious and well worth a try. Smoked eel is also a tremendous delicacy, and surprisingly easy to make.

Finally, I would add that live eels are hard to kill, and harder to skin. After many grisly experiments I have concluded that the best way is to let your fishmonger do it for you.

To Smoke Eels

It is possible to smoke eels in the little smoking boxes which can be purchased at good ironmongers or fishing tackle shops. However, the best method is to use an oil drum which is big enough for the smoke to circulate freely around the hanging eels.

First, find an empty oil drum, and clean it out by setting fire to the inside to burn off all the oil. Make a small fire and surround it with a circle of bricks. Place the drum on top of the bricks, open end upwards. Cover the bottom of the drum with oak sawdust or chips. Gut the eels (don't bother to skin them) and thread coathanger wire through their gills. Rest the ends of the wire over the rim of the drum so that the eels are hanging in the drum, tails well clear of the sawdust.

Cover the drum with a sheet of metal or a paving stone. The oak sawdust will smoulder, releasing smoke and heat which will together cook the eels. Cooking times vary, depending on the heat of the fire and the size of the eel. A minimum of four hours is a good guideline.

This may seem like a lot of trouble, but smoked eel is extremely good and prized by many above smoked salmon.

Grilled Eel

Serves 6

This is one of the simplest ways of cooking eel. Ask your fishmonger to cut the eel into pieces for you.

3 small skinned eels, chopped into 2" pieces
5 tablespoons (5 x 15 ml spoon) each olive oil, lemon juice, wine vinegar
salt and pepper

Tartare Sauce:

½ pint (300 ml) mayonnaise, (see next recipe)
mixed with 1 teaspoon (1 x 5 ml spoon) each of chopped capers, chives, parsley and gherkins

Put the eel pieces into a flat dish. Season well with salt and pepper. Make a marinade with the other ingredients and pour over the pieces. Let this sit for a couple of hours.

Thread coathanger wire through the pieces and rest the wire over the edges of the grill pan, so the fat drips freely away. Grill the eel under a moderate heat, brushing occasionally with the remaining marinade, until the flesh begins to come away from the bone. Place the pieces on a serving dish and serve hot or cold with tartare sauce

Cold Pike with Chive or Cress Mayonnaise

Serves 6

Pike can be found in ponds and rivers in Herefordshire and have been called "the fresh-water wolf", because of their voracious appetite for the smaller fish around them. If you have difficulty obtaining them, ask a local fisherman for help.

Pike have distinctive Y-shaped bones which are easily removed, and the flesh is firm with a delicate flavour. Izaak

Walton describes his favourite way of cooking pike as being "too good a dish for any but anglers , or very honest men". Meanwhile this is Patricia Hegarty's favourite way of eating pike.

1 5 lb (about 2.5 kilos) pike
1 pint (600 ml) white wine

For the Mayonnaise:

2 egg yolks
1/4 pint (150 ml) olive oil
1/4 pint (150 ml) sunflower oil
2 tablespoons (2 x 15 ml spoons) apple vinegar
pinch of salt
For a watercress mayonnaise, add a handful of finely chopped watercress
For a chive mayonnaise, add 2 tablespoons (2 x 15 ml spoons) chopped chives

Cut the head and tail off the pike, lay it on a foil sheet in the roasting pan and pour the wine over it. Seal the parcel and bake for about half an hour or until cooked through, at 375°, Gas Mark 5.

Allow the fish to cool thoroughly. It is then easy to detach the skin and fillet. Divide the fillets into suitable portions. You will find that most of the bones can be gently pulled out from the ends of the sections.

Make the mayonnaise by very slowly adding the oil and then the vinegar to the egg yolks beating vigorously all the while. Add the green herbs of your choice with a pinch of salt at the end.

Spoon a little of the mayonnaise over each portion and garnish with a sprig of cress or freshly chopped chives.

Jenny Allday's Fish Pie

Serves 6

This plain fish pie is easy to make and comes from Jenny Allday, who lives in St. Owens Cross and runs her own catering company.

2 lbs (about 1 kilo) white fish
1 pint (600 ml) milk
1/4 lb (100 g) sliced onions
2 oz (50 g) butter
1 level tablespoon (1 x 15 ml spoon) chopped parsley
1 level tablespoon (1 x 15 ml spoon) chopped fennel
1 clove of garlic chopped finely
1 oz (25 g) flour
juice of half a lemon,l 1 standard tin of tomatoes, well drained
2 oz (50 g) grated cheese (cheddar or Gruyère)
salt and pepper

For the topping:

1 lb (450 g) potatoes mashed with 1 oz (25 g) butter and 6 tablespoons (6 x 15 ml spoon) milk

Simmer the fish in the milk until cooked. Cool, flake and remove the bones. Reserve the liquid. Soften the onions and garlic in the butter. Add the flour and mix to make a roux. Strain the milk from the cooked fish, and use ½ pint (300 ml) of this to make a sauce. Fold the fish into the sauce and add the herbs, salt, pepper and lemon juice. Put the fish mixture into a greased casserole and arrange the tomatoes on top. Top with mashed potatoes and grated cheese. Place in a pre-heated oven at 400°, Gas Mark 6 for 20 minutes until brown on the top.

Poultry and Game

Chicken Breasts with Calvados

Serves 6

This recipe comes from Elly Parker of Effy's Restaurant. Bulmer's have only recently begun to sell a cider brandy of their own, and Elly reckons that it is every bit as good as Calvados in this dish. The brandy cuts through the richness of the cream and butter while the cardamom and sliced apple give the chicken an exotic, fruity taste. I have allowed one chicken breast per person.

6 chicken breasts off the bone
3 oz (75 g) unsalted butter
2 teaspoons (2 x 5 ml spoons) freshly ground cardamom
3 apples peeled and sliced carefully just before using
6 tablespoons (6 x 15 ml spoons) cider brandy
6 tablespoons (6 x 15 ml spoons) cream
salt and pepper

Melt the butter in a large frying pan. Add the chicken breasts and cook lightly on both sides. Then add the cardamom and salt and pepper. Add the sliced apple and cook carefully so that the slices retain their shape. Pour over the brandy and bring to bubbling point. Remove from the heat. Put the chicken breasts and the apple slices on a warmed plate or serving dish. Return the pan with juices to the heat and add the cream. Swirl to a boil, and pour over and around the chicken.

Chicken with Prunes

Serves 6 - 8

In 1867 the Honourable Lady Llanover collected a series of recipes "communicated by the Welsh hermit of the cell of St. Gower with various remarks on many things past and present." These recipes were apparently chalked up on the door of the hermit's cell, and Lady Llanover wrote them down. Among them was a recipe for chicken, prunes and leeks. The version below seems to have lost the leeks when it crossed the border into Herefordshire, gaining the hazelnuts and cider instead.

1 5 lb (about 2.5 kilos) chicken
18 prunes, stoned
½ pint (300 ml) dry cider
18 hazelnuts
salt and pepper

Soak the prunes in the cider for 12 hours. Remove the prunes and stuff each one with a hazelnut. Keep the cider. Salt the inside of the chicken and stuff with the prunes. Tie up the legs. Pour a couple of tablespoons of cider into the bottom of a heavy casserole dish. Put in the chicken, and bake in a heavy pot for 1½ hours at 300°, Gas Mark 3, or until tender. Remove the chicken from the pot to a warmed serving dish. Pour off any excess fat. Add the remaining cider, and reduce the gravy slightly. Season to taste. Strain and serve the gravy separately.

Country Cooks' Chicken

Serves 6

This recipe comes from Jenny Allday. It is a substantial chicken stew eaten with a side dish of fried apple.

1 3½ lb (1.75 kilos) chicken
1½ lbs (700 g) dessert apples

4 oz (100 g) mushrooms sliced
4 oz (100 g) bacon diced
1/2 pint (300 ml) dry cider
2 onions
4 carrots
3 oz (75 g) butter
1 tablespoon (1 x 15 ml spoon) vegetable oil
Bouquet garni
salt and pepper
3/4 pint (450 ml) water

Joint the chicken and put the pieces to one side. Put the carcase in a saucepan and cover with the water. Add salt, pepper, bouquet garni, an onion and the carrots. Simmer for 1½ hours to make a stock. Strain and reduce to a quarter pint.

Heat the oil and half the butter in a heavy saucepan and brown the chicken pieces quickly. Remove from the pan and soften the onion with the diced bacon. Put them with the chicken in a casserole dish. Lightly sauté the mushrooms and add to the chicken. Heat the cider and pour over the chicken. Cook with the lid on in a preheated oven, 375°, Gas Mark 5, for 45 minutes until the chicken is tender. Add the reduced stock and adjust the seasoning.

Ten minutes before serving, dice the apples and fry them quickly in the remaining butter. Serve them beside the chicken.

Elizabeth Foley's Stuffed Chicken

Serves 6 - 8

The original recipe calls for "cockcombs, truffles, and morralls" to be added to the chicken. I have substituted large open mushrooms. Field mushrooms would be ideal.

1 4 lb (almost 2 kilos) fresh chicken with giblets
1 onion stuck with two cloves
1 tablespoon (1 x 15 ml spoon) sunflower oil
1 rasher streaky bacon

5 anchovy fillets finely chopped
1/4 pint (150 ml) strong chicken stock
1/4 pint (150 ml) red wine
2 tablespoons (2 x 15 ml spoons) chopped fresh herbs
salt and pepper

For the stuffing:

6 oz (150 g) white breadcrumbs
2 small onions
2 rashers streaky bacon
1 chicken liver from the giblets
1 dessertspoon (1 x 10 ml spoon) lemon juice
1 tablespoon (1 x 15 ml spoon) lemon rind
3 tablespoons (3 x 15 ml spoons) chopped fresh mixed herbs
1 egg
salt and pepper

Put all the giblets except the liver into a saucepan with water and boil for forty - five minutes. Reduce to a quarter of a pint, strain and reserve. For the stuffing, melt the butter in a saucepan and soften the chopped onion. Mince the chicken liver and streaky bacon together. Add the breadcrumbs to the softened onions and mix well. Add the lemon juice and rind and the chopped herbs. Mix together and add the minced meat and the egg. Season with salt and pepper. Stuff the chicken with this mixture and tie the legs together securely.

Put the sunflower oil in a heavy frying pan and brown the chicken on all sides, turning it carefully. Transfer the chicken to a large casserole dish and add the reduced stock, wine, anchovies, the onion stuck with cloves, and the rasher of bacon, cut into pieces. Season with salt and pepper. Cook slowly in an oven preheated to 300°, Gas Mark 3, for 1 1/4 hours. Half an hour before the chicken is ready, add the mushrooms. When the chicken is cooked, put it on a warm serving dish with the mushrooms around it. Strain the gravy, check for seasoning and serve separately.

Chicken Pie

Serves 6 - 8
The idea for this recipe comes from Elizabeth Foley. However, as she is rather vague and doesn't give a complete list of ingredients, I have incorporated parts of a traditional recipe from the inimitable Mrs. Beeton.

8 oz (225 g) flaky pastry
1 4 - 5 lb (over 2 kilos) chicken with giblets
1/2 pint (300 ml) chicken stock
good pinch ground nutmeg
good pinch ground mace
salt and pepper
bouquet garni
1 onion

For the forcemeat:

4 oz (100 g) suet
2 oz (50 g) minced bacon
6 oz (150 g) breadcrumbs
grated rind of half a lemon
2 eggs
1 dessertspoon (1 x 10 ml spoon) chopped parsley
1 dessertspoon (1 x 10 ml spoon) chopped thyme and marjoram
salt and cayenne pepper

Make a stock by boiling the carcase and neck of the chicken in a saucepan of water with the onion and bouquet garni and salt. Simmer for one and a half hours and reduce to amount required. Make the forcemeat by mixing the breadcrumbs, bacon, suet, lemon peel and herbs with the egg. Season well and shape into balls.

Skin and joint the chicken pieces. Take a deep pie dish and put a layer of chicken pieces in the bottom, then a layer of forcemeat balls. Lightly season each layer with nutmeg, mace, salt and pepper. Repeat this process until the dish is full, then carefully pour over the strained stock. Roll out the pastry and and cover the pie. Bake at 425°, Gas Mark 7 for 10 minutes, then reduce to 350°, Gas Mark 4, for a further 1¼ hours.

Pigeon Casserole

Serves 6

Anyone who has a vegetable garden knows about pigeons. This recipe provides an opportunity for getting your own back. They are delicious, as one would expect given their diet of tender green plants. Allow one pigeon per person.

6 young pigeons
¾ lb (350 g) button onions
3 tablespoons (3 x 15 ml spoons) oil
1 tablespoon (1 x 15 ml spoon) flour
1 pint (600 ml) dry cider
grated rind and juice of an orange
1 tablespoon (1 x 15 ml spoon) redcurrant jelly
½ lb (225 g) chestnuts peeled and skinned
salt and pepper
chopped parsley

Cut each pigeon in half along the breastbone and trim off the backbone and wings to leave just the breast and the thick part of the leg. Heat the oil in a large pan, and brown the onions and pigeon pieces. Put them in a large casserole dish. Stir the flour into the remaining oil in the pan and cook for 1 minute. Add the cider, orange rind and juice and redcurrant jelly and bring to the boil, stirring all the time. Simmer for 2 minutes and pour over the pigeons. Add the chestnuts. Season with salt and pepper. Cover and cook in an oven preheated to 300°, Gas Mark 3, for about two hours or more until tender. Sprinkle with parsley before serving.

Pigeon with Lovage

Serves 6

Lovage is thought to have been introduced to Britain by the Romans. It was very popular in medieval herb gardens, and looks rather like a giant celery plant with a lemony, celery-like taste. Patricia Hegarty uses it with perry in this distinctive pigeon casserole.

6 plump pigeons
2 tablespoons (2 x 15 ml spoons) sunflower oil
1 medium onion chopped
2 pints (1.2 litres) dry Perry
small bunch of lovage
salt and pepper
dash of tamari
2 teaspoons (2 x 5 ml spoons) cornflour

Brown the pigeons in the oil. Put them head down in a casserole. Add the onion and cover the pigeons with the perry. If necessary top up with a little water. Tuck a few lovage leaves down the side of the pot. Cook slowly at 300°, Gas Mark 3, for 2 hours or more until the birds are really tender. Take out and cool. Keep about 1 pint (600 ml) of the cooking stock warm in the casserole. Strain the remainder and reduce it to about half a pint. Taste, and add a few more lovage leaves if you like it stronger. Thicken with the cornflour. Strain. Season with salt and pepper and a dash of tamari for taste as well as colour.

Take the breasts off the pigeons and replace them in the casserole with the remaining stock to warm in the oven at about 200°, Gas Mark 1. When ready to serve, quickly drain each breast on a piece of kitchen paper, spoon over the hot sauce and garnish with a bright green lovage leaf.

Cider Rabbit Stew

Serves 6 - 8

Rabbit used to be the only meat that many people in Herefordshire ever tasted. It was also eaten in great quantities in the servants' halls of the county's great houses. Most good butchers keep rabbit - it is slightly meatier than chicken, and well worth a try. This recipe calls for cider and cider brandy, though the brandy is strictly optional!

1 young rabbit cut into joints
3 medium onions, finely sliced
2 tablespoons (2 x 15 ml spoons) chopped fresh thyme, basil, and marjoram
1 tablespoon (1 x 15 ml spoon) chopped parsley
2 oz (50 g) butter or margarine
½ pint (225 ml) dry cider
3 tablespoons (3 x 15 ml spoons) cider brandy
salt and pepper
seasoned flour

For the forcemeat balls:

heart and liver of the rabbit
4 oz (100 g) streaky bacon
4 oz (100 g) white breadcrumbs
2 oz (50 g) prepared suet
1 tablespoon (1 x 15 ml spoon) chopped fresh herbs as above
1 tablespoon (1 x 15 ml spoon) chopped parsley
1 dessertspoon (1 x 10 ml spoon) grated lemon rind
1 egg
salt and pepper

Roll the rabbit joints in seasoned flour. Melt the butter and brown the chopped onion in a casserole. Add the rabbit joints and brown on all sides. Add the herbs and the cider and cider brandy (if used). Season with salt and pepper. Simmer in a low oven, 250° - 275°, Gas Mark 1 - 2, for 2 hours or until tender.

Meanwhile make the forcemeat balls by mincing together the liver and heart of the rabbit with the streaky bacon. Mix this with the breadcrumbs, suet, herbs, lemon rind and egg. Season with salt and pepper. Form into small balls and sauté gently. Spoon these carefully into the casserole five minutes before taking it out of the oven. Check the seasoning and serve.

Because of the uncertainty as to cooking time - a young rabbit takes a shorter time than an older one - it is a good idea to cook the rabbit the day before, and then add the forcemeat balls after it has been thoroughly reheated.

A Venison "Pasty"

Serves 6

The original of this recipe is in Elizabeth Foley's book. Most of the venison in Herefordshire comes from fallow and red deer from large estates in the county. The season varies for different deer, but on the whole bucks are eaten from August to April, and does from November to February. Most butchers hang the meat for two weeks before it is sold, and venison should always be marinated for at least two days before it is cooked.

2 lbs (almost 1 kilo) cubed meat and kidney (for a less gamey flavour omit the kidney)
2 small onions diced
1 teaspoon (1 x 2.5 ml spoon) ground mace
1 teaspoon (1 x 2.5 ml spoon) ground nutmeg
2 teaspoons (2 x 5 ml spoons) salt
1 oz (25 g) flour
3 oz (75 g) butter
1/2 pint (300 ml) cider
pepper
8 oz (225 g) puff pastry
1 beaten egg

Marinate the meat in the cider for two days. Melt the butter in a heavy casserole and soften the onions. Strain the meat from the cider and fry it with the softened onion. Stir in the flour and add the spices, salt and pepper. Add the cider and mix well. Cook covered, in an oven preheated to 300°, Gas Mark 3, for 2 hours, until the meat is really tender. Allow to cool overnight.

Put the cooked meat in the bottom of a pie dish. Roll out the pastry, cut a long strip and put it round the rim of the pie dish. Moisten with water and press down the pie lid firmly. Brush the edges with beaten egg to seal them. Make a hole in the centre and decorate with pastry leaves. Brush the top with egg and chill for two hours. Preheat the oven to 450°, Gas Mark 8. Cook the pie for 20 - 30 minutes until the crust is high and crisp and brown. Reduce the heat slightly if the top begins to burn. Serve hot or cold.

Meat

Lamb with Port

Serves 6 - 8

This recipe comes from a little cookery book, written by Maria Ballard, the great grandmother of Patricia Hegarty. Maria Ballard was married to Stephen Ballard, the engineer who was responsible for the building of the Hereford - Worcester railway and the Ledbury Viaduct.

According to Patricia, Mrs. Ballard was an abstemious woman both inside and outside her kitchen. However, in this recipe she has thrown caution to the winds and the result is delicious. If port is not available, a wineglass of red wine and a tablespoon of redcurrant jelly could be substituted.

1 5 lb (about 2.5 kilos) leg of lamb
1 large onion stuck with 2 cloves
2 tablespoons (2 x 15 ml spoons) walnut ketchup
4 anchovies cut into small pieces
bunch of sweet herbs (basil, tarragon, marjoram etc.)
1 wineglass of port
(or 1 wineglass of red wine and 1 tablespoon (1 x 15 ml spoon) redcurrant jelly)
good pinch nutmeg
salt and pepper
1 teaspoon (1 x 5 ml spoon) cornflour

Skin the leg of lamb and season it with nutmeg, salt and pepper. Put in a casserole dish with the onion, ketchup, port (or wine and redcurrant jelly), anchovies and the herbs finely chopped. Cover and stew gently for 2½ hours in an oven preheated to 300°, Gas Mark 3. When the meat is tender, remove it to a warm serving dish. Skim off any fat in the gravy, strain it and thicken it with the cornflour. Bring to the boil to cook the cornflour, and serve separately.

Hope End Lamb Noisettes

Serves 6

For over 400 years the production of pears for perry making has played a vital part in the economy of Herefordshire. The orchards had their heyday in the late seventeenth and early eighteenth century, but began a long decline following the Industrial Revolution and, later, competition from commercially produced beer and soft drinks.

Perry pear trees grow to an enormous size and can live for 300 years. The largest tree on record spreads itself over 1¾ acres! It is partly due to this longevity that perry making has survived into the twentieth century.

Perry pears have wonderful names like Merrylegs, Mumblehead and Lumberskull which sound more like a description of a perry drinker than the pear itself!

This recipes allows two noisettes per person. Patricia Hegarty uses a pure perry which comes from Dunkerton's.

12 lamb noisettes
2 tablespoons (2 x 15 ml spoons) meat juices
1 oz (25 g) fine wholemeal flour
½ pint (300 ml) perry
dash of tamari
redcurrant jelly
sprig rosemary
salt and pepper

Bone the cutlets. Remove the central fillet, carefully taking with it most of the fat along the cutlet, so that you are left with a thin strip. Bind this neatly round the meat and secure with two cocktail sticks. Put the bones and scraps into a roasting pan and extract the juices by roasting it at 350°, Gas Mark 4, for about 45 minutes. Make a roux by mixing the flour with the fat and juices extracted from the roasting pan. Add the perry to make a sauce. Season with salt and pepper. Add the rosemary and a dash of tamari. Cook for five minutes. Strain and set aside.

Grill the noisettes under a high heat for about twelve minutes, turning occasionally. Remove the cocktail sticks and serve with the sauce and a garnish of redcurrant jelly.

Harigo Lamb

Serves 6

This was originally a recipe for mutton. I have updated it and it makes a good honest summery stew.

Local butchers tell me that, on the whole, demand for mutton faded away in the late 1950s and early 1960s. According to Mrs. Iris Jones, it formed the staple diet of the staff at Garnons. Between the wars so many of the female staff produced twins that it was commonly believed there must have been something in the mutton! *3 lbs (1.5 kilos) best end of neck lamb chops*

1 dessertspoon (1 x 10 ml spoon) sunflower oil
6 medium sized carrots chopped into rounds
3 turnips peeled, and chopped
1 large hearted lettuce or 2 small ones
1 teaspoon (1 x 5 ml spoon) dried or chopped fresh thyme
3 stalks celery, chopped
3/4 pint (450 ml) boiling light stock or water
cayenne pepper
salt

Heat the oil in a heavy casserole. Brown the meat lightly on both sides. Pour in the boiling stock or water. Add the carrots and cook gently uncovered for fifteen minutes. Add the turnips, celery, thyme, and the lettuce roughly chopped. Season well with salt and cayenne pepper to taste. Simmer covered for 1¼ hours or until tender. Check seasoning and serve.

Lamb Steaks in Puff Pastry

These lamb steaks come from Effy's Restaurant. The secret to the success of the pastry is to put it straight from a cold refrigerator into a very hot oven. The proportions given are per person, and the ingredients should be made in advance - which makes them handy for a dinner party!

Per person:

1 6 - 8 oz (175 - 225 g) lamb steak
3 - 4 oz (75 - 100 g) rolled out square of puff pastry
beaten yolk of an egg

For the stuffing:

Per steak:
4 oz (100 g) unsalted butter
3 mushrooms chopped
half a small clove of garlic diced
2 heaped tablespoons (2 x 15 ml spoons) breadcrumbs
salt and pepper

Mix all the stuffing by hand and work in the butter gradually. Spread some of the stuffing on the pastry square and the rest on the lamb steak. Wrap the pastry round the meat and seal by brushing the inside edges with egg yolk then pressing together. Brush more egg yolk over the top. Chill. Place in a hot oven, thoroughly preheated to 450°, Gas Mark 8, for ten minutes. Check after seven minutes that the pastry isn't burning.

These delicious parcels can be kept warm for up to half an hour before serving.

Collared Breast of Lamb with Onion Sauce

Serves 4

This is a very economical dish which comes from Anne Ward's cookery book. It could be cooked in advance, sliced and heated up in the oven with the onion sauce poured over the top.

1 boned breast of lamb
a good handful each of fresh thyme, marjoram and parsley
2 shallots
1 egg yolk
salt and pepper

For the stock:

1 onion
1 carrot
4 peppercorns
water

For the Sauce:

1 medium onion, diced
1 oz (25 g) butter
1 oz (25 g) flour
½ pint (300 ml) stock
½ pint (300 ml) milk
salt and pepper
1 dessertspoon (1 x 10 ml spoon) white wine vinegar

Spread out the breast and cut off any gristle or hard fatty bits. Rub over with the egg yolk and season with salt and pepper. Finely chop the herbs and shallots and spread over the meat. Roll up tightly and tie with tape. Put into a large saucepan with the onion, carrot and peppercorns. Cover with boiling water and simmer very gently for about 2 hours or until tender.

Make the onion sauce by softening the onion in the butter, then stir in the flour. Add some of the hot stock from the meat, and then the milk. Stir until thick and creamy. Season with salt and pepper; lastly, add the vinegar. Slice the lamb and serve with the onion sauce poured over the top.

Roast Pork with Thyme

Serves 8

This way of cooking the traditional joint makes a pleasant change and is good hot or cold

1 5 lb (2.5 kilos) piece of pork
1 lemon
good handful of fresh thyme finely chopped
2 cloves of garlic finely chopped
3 tablespoons (3 x 15 ml spoons) olive oil
salt and pepper

Grate the lemon rind and squeeze the juice. Mix the rind with half the thyme and one clove of garlic. Make deep cuts in the meat and push this mixture inside. Score the skin with a sharp knife. In a small bowl mix the oil, lemon juice, the remainder of the thyme and the chopped garlic. Season well. Rub this mixture over the meat. Preheat the oven to 350°, Gas Mark 5, and place the meat, fat side up, in a roasting pan. Allow 35 - 45 minutes per pound. Fifteen minmutes before the end of cooking time, turn up the heat to 425°, Gas Mark 7, to crispen the crackling.

Brisket with Orange

Serves 6 - 8

This recipe combines orange, allspice and angostura bitters to make a special dish out of a piece of brisket or any stewing beef. The brisket may be used frozen, in which case the cooking time is 4 hours at 250°, Gas Mark 1.

1 3-4 lb (about 1.75 kilos) piece of brisket
2 large onions, sliced
1 tablespoon (1 x 15 ml spoon) sunflower oil
3 oranges
1/2 pint (300 ml) dry cider
1/2 pint (300 ml) stock
2 teaspoons (2 x 5 ml spoons) angostura bitters
good pinch of allspice
2 teaspoons (2 x 5 ml spoons) cornflour
salt and pepper
3 tablespoons (3 x 15 ml spoons) unsweetened yoghurt

Heat the oil in a heavy casserole dish. Sauté the onions and set aside. Put in the brisket and brown on all sides. Peel the rind from one of the oranges and put in a saucepan with the cider, stock, juice of the orange, angostura bitters and the allspice. Return the onions to the casserole. Heat the stock to boiling and pour over the brisket. Season with salt and pepper. Cover the dish and cook very gently for 2 hours at 275°-300°, Gas Mark 2. Allow the beef to cool overnight. (This makes it easier to cut into slices.)

Next day remove the beef from the stock and cut into slices. Cut the remaining oranges into thin slices. Arrange the meat and orange slices in alternate layers down the centre of a shallow serving dish. Strain the stock and reduce it by half. Thicken with the cornflour. Pour the sauce over the beef and orange slices. Closely cover the dish with tinfoil and thoroughly reheat in an oven, 325°, Gas Mark 3. Immediately before serving, when the sauce is bubbling hot, spoon a sash of yoghurt down the middle of the slices.

Hereford Beef Olives

Serves 6

On Wednesday October 30th 1878 Edith Victor walked two miles into Hereford to attend her second cooking class but discovered it was so well attended that she could not get a good seat; besides, she declares in her diary, " boiled fowl was not an appetising proceeding to look at. "

The next Wednesday she fared better. " I got very good seats and saw and heard well both apple fritters and Beef Olives.

The recipe below uses prime Hereford beef and has been made famous by Patricia Hegarty.

1 2 lb (about 1 kilo) piece of topside
8 oz (225 g) thinly - cut green back rashers
8 oz (225 g) ripe tomatoes, peeled and quartered
olive oil
1 pint (600 ml) dry cider
stock or water
2 level teaspoons (2 x 5 ml spoons) cornflour

Stuffing:

2 oz (50 g) brown breadcrumbs
1 medium onion grated
zest and juice of half a lemon
1 level teaspoon (1 x 5 ml spoon) finely chopped fresh thyme
1 level teaspoon (1 x 5 ml spoon) finely chopped fresh marjoram
1 egg yolk
2 level tablespoons (2 x 15 ml spoons) tomato paste
sea salt and pepper
wooden cocktail sticks

Chill the beef in the coldest part of the refrigerator or freezer until you can cut it into thin slices, measuring roughly 2" x 4" - 5cm x 10cm . Blanch the bacon for two minutes in boiling water. Gently cook the tomatoes in their own juice, and sieve. Combine the stuffing ingredients to make a crumbly thick paste (brown breadcrumbs are just right for this). Lay a strip of bacon along the inside of each slice of beef. Spread stuffing on the bacon, roll up and secure with a cocktail stick. This can all be done in advance. Switch on the oven to 300°, Gas Mark 2-3. Brown the 'olives' in olive oil, then put them in a casserole dish. Pour off the surplus fat from the pan. Mix the tomato paste with the cider and pour over the beef. Add any scraps left over, with more stock or water if necessary. Cover with a lid for an hour and cook until tender.

Remove the 'olives'. Strain the liquor into a wide, shallow pan and boil down to about ¾ pint (½ litre). Thicken the sauce with cornflour and season to taste. Remove the cocktail sticks, arrange the 'olives' in a row on a serving dish and spoon the sauce over the top.

Effyburgers

Serves 4

These versatile meatballs come from Effy's Restaurant.
They can be flattened and used for hamburgers or rolled into small balls, fried, and stuffed into envelopes of pitta bread with slices of cucumber, tomato and onion.

1 lb (450 g) good minced beef
½ lb (225 g) pork sausage meat
1 clove of garlic
1 small onion
1 dessertspoon (1 x 10 ml spoon) mustard powder
1 egg
a good bunch of sage, parsley, thyme, marjoram
salt and pepper

Put everything except the mince and sausage meat into a food processor and mix for a couple of minutes. Alternatively, finely dice the garlic, onion and herbs. Pound these with the egg, mustard powder and salt and pepper in a small bowl. Mix the two meats together lightly, add the seasoning and mix by hand. Too much handling spoils the consistency of the meatballs. Form into hamburgers or meatballs as desired. Fry in a heavy frying pan with a little sunflower oil.

Light lunches and suppers

Anne Ward's Red Cabbage

Serves 6

This recipe is especially good with pork and game, and can be eaten hot or cold. For a more substantial dish, half a dozen finely chopped bacon rashers could be added with the onion. It takes quite a long time to cook, but is well worth waiting for.

1 red cabbage weighing about 2½ lbs (just over 1 kilo)
3 oz (75 g) butter
2 medium onions finely chopped
3 tart apples, peeled and sliced
6 tablespoons (6 x 15 ml spoon) red wine vinegar
2 tablespoons (2 x 15 ml spoon) honey
1 teaspoon (1 x 5 ml spoon) caraway seeds
1 teaspoon (1 x 5 ml spoon) salt

Cut the cabbage into thin slices and soak in a large bowl of cold water. Meanwhile melt the butter in a casserole dish and soften the onions. Lift the cabbage from the water without draining it, and put it into a large pot or iron casserole with the onions. Simmer gently for ten minutes. Peel and slice the apples and add to the cabbage. Add the caraway seeds, salt, vinegar and honey. Stir gently and simmer very slowly for 1¼ hours until all the water has been absorbed. (Check from time to time that the water hasn't evaporated too soon, or the cabbage will burn).

Spinach and Sorrel Soufflé

Serves 6

This recipe comes from Ros Fry, who lives near Hay-on-Wye. Ros is a professional cook and cookery demonstrator and she specializes in vegetarian food.

½ lb (225 g) sorrel
½ lb (225 g) spinach
2 oz (50 g) butter
2 oz (50 g) flour
½ pint (300 ml) milk
½ teaspoon (1 x 2.5 ml spoon) dried mustard
2 oz (50 g) strong cheddar or Gruyère cheese
4 eggs
1 dessertspoon (1 x 10 ml spoon) parmesan cheese
1 oz (25 g) breadcrumbs
pinch of cayenne pepper
salt and pepper

Wash the spinach and sorrel carefully, and remove any tough stalks. Blanch in salted water for two minutes. Drain well and allow to cool slightly. Squeeze out as much moisture as possible. Chop the mixture very finely, or use a food processor. Butter a 6" soufflé dish and sprinkle the sides with breadcrumbs - this allows the soufflé to "climb" the sides of the dish.

Melt the butter in a heavy pan and stir in the flour to form a roux. Remove from the heat and add the milk in a continuous stream, stirring all the time. Return the saucepan to the heat and bring the sauce to the boil, stirring constantly. If the mixture looks lumpy, whisk it briskly with a hand whisk until smooth. Remove from the heat again and add the salt, pepper, cayenne, mustard, cheddar or Gruyère cheese, and finally the spinach and sorrel. Mix well and allow to cool.

Separate the eggs and beat the yolks into the sauce one by one. Whisk the egg whites until stiff but not dry. Mix a spoonful of white into the sorrel mixture to loosen it, then fold in the rest gently but quickly. Pour the mixture into the soufflé dish. (It should be about two-thirds full). Cut through the mixture several times with a knife to release any large air pockets. Sprinkle the top with parmesan cheese, and bake in a hot oven pre- set to 400°, Gas Mark 6, for 25 minutes. The soufflé should be moist in the middle, but crisp at the edges. Serve immediately.

Pasta with Broad Beans

Serves 4

This recipe is quick and simple to make and most economical when broad beans are growing in the garden.

1 lb (450 g) pasta shells
1/2 lb (225 g) broad beans, shelled
1/4 pint (150 ml) cream
2 eggs
5 anchovies, finely chopped
1/2 oz (15 g) butter
salt and pepper

Cook the pasta shells in plenty of boiling salted water. Boil the broad beans for four or five minutes, until tender but not mushy. Strain, add butter and put to one side. Pour the cream into a bowl and add the eggs and the anchovies. Season well and mix thoroughly. When the pasta is cooked, drain and rinse well with boiling water. Add the beans to the pasta and pour over the cream mixture, stirring all the time. Serve immediately.

Pasta with Walnut Sauce

Serves 4

This sauce is an original from Effy's restaurant. It is light and unusual and especially good with homemade pasta.

1lb (450 g) pasta
8oz (225 g) cream cheese
1/4 pint (150 ml) cream
3 oz (75 g) chopped walnuts
salt and pepper
parmesan cheese

Put the cream cheese and the cream in a saucepan and cook very slowly for 10 minutes - do not allow to boil. When the sauce is thick, add the chopped walnuts and season well with salt and pepper. While the sauce is cooking, cook the pasta in plenty of boiling water to which salt and a dash of oil have been added. When the pasta is cooked, drain it and rinse it with boiling water to remove excess starch. Toss the pasta in the sauce and serve with a bowl of parmesan cheese. A most delicious meal with a fresh green salad.

Puddings

Orange Pudding

Serves 8

This is one of Elizabeth Foley's recipes; she calls it "Orange Puden". The original calls for "a grated penny loaf" and more y^{n} ½ a pound of sugar." I have altered the proportions to suit an age with a less sweet tooth. The "puden" is delicious eaten hot or cold with cream.

8 oz (225 g) puff pastry
3 medium oranges
6 oz (175 g) butter
6 oz (175 g) sugar
4 egg yolks plus 1 white
3 tablespoons (3 x 15 ml spoons) cream
5 oz (125 g) white breadcrumbs

Grate the peel off the oranges, chop up the fruit and remove the pith. Mash them both together. Cream the butter and sugar. Add the yolks one at a time. Put in the breadcrumbs and the orange pulp. Finally add the cream and mix thoroughly.

Roll out the puff pastry and cut a long strip to put around the rim of the pie dish, allowing it to drop down the inside slightly. This will form the base to seal the pastry cover. Spoon in the orange mixture. Brush the pastry rim with egg white. Lay the remaining pastry over the top to form a lid, and press down the edges to seal it. Make a central hole and brush the lid with egg white. Preheat the oven to 450°, Gas Mark 8, and cook for 25 - 30 minutes. Reduce the heat slightly if the top begins to burn.

Ginger Ice Cream

Serves 8

At the turn of the century *The Hereford Times* introduced a Ladies' Page, which included articles on all aspects of a lady's life from the correct management and care of children, to the way to decorate an Easter bonnet. This recipe appeared in January 1908. It is easy to make and tastes delicious.

1½ pints (900 ml) good custard
2 oz (50 g) preserved ginger cut up small
2 tablespoons (2 x 15 ml spoons) syrup from the preserved ginger
½ pint (300 ml) whipped cream

Mix all the ingredients together and freeze.

Raspberry and Redcurrant Pie

Serves 8

In July 1808, James Ely decided to take the stagecoach from his home in Thornbury, Gloucestershire, and return to Leominster where he was born. It was a nostalgic journey, and he mentions stopping in Hereford where he ate a raspberry and redcurrant pie.

Pastry

12 oz (350 g) flour
2 tablespoons (2 x 15 ml spoons) icing sugar
8 oz (225 g) butter
1 egg yolk

pinch of salt
cold water to mix
Pastry Glaze: *1 egg white*
caster sugar

Filling:

12 oz (350 g) raspberries
4 oz (100 g) redcurrants topped and tailed
4 oz (100 g) sugar or more to taste
1/4 pint (150 ml) double cream
3 tablespoons (3 x 15 ml spoons) single cream
2 egg yolks

Line a pie dish with slightly over half the pastry. Brush with egg white, and sprinkle over the caster sugar to cover the base. Put in the raspberries and redcurrants and the rest of the sugar. Make a lid for the pie with the remaining pastry, and cut a hole in the centre, big enough to fit the stem of a small funnel. Press the edges together, brush over with egg white and sprinkle lightly with caster sugar. Preheat the oven to 375°, Gas Mark 5, and bake for 40 - 45 minutes.

About five minutes before the end of cooking time when the pastry looks done, pour the two creams into a saucepan and heat them to boiling point. Take off the heat and pour them over the egg yolks, beating hard all the time. Remove the pie from the oven and carefully pour this custard mixture through the funnel and into the central hole. Do this slowly so it does not overflow. Put the pie back in the oven for another five minutes. Let the pie sit for fifteen minutes after it has been taken from the oven to give the custard a chance to thicken. This pie should be eaten warm and does not need more cream.

Leominster Custard Pie

Serves 6

Mr. James Ely must have been a rather portly gentleman. At any rate, he seems to have been very fond of his food and writes that when he arrived in Leominster at the end of his journey, he dined off a leg of lamb with peas, followed by a Leominster custard pie.

8 oz (225 g) shortcrust pastry

Filling:

3/4 pint (450 ml) single cream
1 stick cinnamon
2 small blades mace
2 eggs and 2 yolks
2 oz (50 g) sugar
grated nutmeg

Roll out the pastry and line a pie dish with a removable base. Line this with foil and weight it down with dried beans. Bake blind at 400°, Gas Mark 6, for 12 minutes. Take out and remove the foil and beans. Prick the base and bake for a further five minutes. Put the cream in a saucepan with the mace and cinnamon and bring it to the boil. Beat the eggs and the yolks together with the sugar. Pour the scalded cream over this mixture, beating well all the time. Pour the mixture into the pastry case, and sprinkle with a little nutmeg. Reduce the heat of the oven and bake at 325°, Gas Mark 3 - 4, for 35 minutes or until the custard is set. Allow the pie to cool to let the custard thicken.

Ginger Pear Upside Down Pudding

Serves 6

This can be eaten as a cake or as a pudding served hot with whipped cream.

Topping:

1½ oz (35 g) butter
1½ oz (35 g) brown sugar
good pinch ground ginger
3 pears
a few glacé cherries

Sponge:

4 oz (100 g) butter
4 oz (100 g) sugar
4 oz (100 g) self raising flour
2 eggs

Melt the butter and pour into a sponge tin. Sprinkle in the brown sugar and the ginger. Peel, halve and core the pears and arrange in the tin cut side down. Put in the cherries. Make a sponge mixture and pour it over the top of the pear mixture. Bake for 30 minutes in a preheated oven at 350°, Gas Mark 5. Allow the cake to cool for a few minutes, cut around the outside with a sharp knife, and invert onto a serving plate. Decorate with piped whipped cream when the cake is cool enough not to melt it.

Orange and Lemon Cream

Serves 8

Elizabeth Foley had recipes for both Lemon and Orange Creams in her book. The Lemon Cream used all egg whites, while the Orange Cream used all egg yolks. I decided to put the two together, allowing the orange cream to cool in the bottom of a glass bowl, then spreading it with a layer of whipped cream, and finally adding the lemon mixture on the top. It was delicious, and should be eaten with sponge biscuits or macaroons.

For the Orange Cream:

4 medium oranges

6 egg yolks
3 oz (75 g) sugar
water

For the Lemon Cream:

4 lemons
6 egg whites
3 oz (75 g) sugar
water
1/2 pint (300 ml) whipping cream

First make the orange cream. Grate the orange peel and squeeze out all the juice. Add any of the pulp you can salvage from the orange. Weigh this mixture; it should be roughly 12 fl oz. Add the same amount of water to it. Separate the eggs, and beat the yolks with the sugar. Heat the orange juice and water almost to boiling point. Tip a little of this into the egg mixture, beating all the time, then pour it all back into the orange and water mixture. Place the saucepan over, not in, another pan filled with boiling water over heat, and stir constantly until it begins to thicken. This will take a little while. When it is quite thick and coats the back of a spoon, remove it from the heat. Continue stirring for a few minutes to release any steam so the cream does not go watery. Pour it into a glass bowl and let it cool. Chill for a couple of hours.

Whip the cream until stiff and carefully spread it over the cold orange mixture. Chill again.

For the lemon cream, grate the lemon, then squeeze out all the juice. Measure the juice and peel and add to it the same amount of water. Lightly whip the egg whites and gradually add the sugar. Place this mixture over rapidly boiling water and continue beating. Add the lemon water in a slow, steady stream. Beat for ten to fifteen minutes. Remove from heat and beat until the cream has a good frothy consistency. Allow to cool. Spoon this mixture over the whipped cream and refrigerate for a couple of hours before serving.

Whip the cream until stiff and carefully spread it over the cold orange mixture. Chill again.

For the lemon cream, grate the lemon, then squeeze out all the juice. Measure the juice and peel and add to it the same amount of water. Lightly whip the egg whites and gradually add the sugar. Place this mixture over rapidly boiling water and continue beating. Add the lemon water in a slow, steady stream. Beat for ten to fifteen minutes. Remove from heat and beat until the cream has a good frothy consistency. Allow to cool. Spoon this mixture over the whipped cream and refrigerate for a couple of hours before serving.

Hope End Pear and Chestnut Flan

Serves 6

This recipe comes from Patricia Hegarty whose house, Hope End, was Elizabeth Barrett Browning's childhood home. Some lines from one of her poems, "Hector in the Garden," inspired this delicious flan.

Underneath the chestnuts dripping,
Through the grasses wet and fair,
Straight I sought my garden-ground
With the laurel on the mound,
And the pear-tree over-sweeping
A side show on the ground.

Pastry:

3 oz (75 g) fine wholemeal flour
1½ oz (35 g) butter
tablespoon (1 x 15 ml spoon) cold water

Filling:

3 - 4 medium dessert pears, peeled, cored and halved
3/4 pint (450 ml) dry perry
4 oz (100 g) dried chestnuts soaked overnight
vanilla pod
3 tablespoons (3 x 15 ml spoons) honey
Glaze:
1 tablespoon redcurrant or apple jelly

Make the pastry by hand or in a food processor. Chill for 30 minutes then roll out thinly and line a 9" (23 cm) fluted flan tin. Line this with foil and weight it down with dried beans. Bake blind at 400°, Gas Mark 6, for 10 minutes. Take out and remove the foil and beans. Prick the base and bake for a further 5 minutes. Allow to cool.

Poach the pears in the perry until just cooked. Lift out carefully with a slotted spoon and allow to cool. Simmer the chestnuts and vanilla pod in the same liquor until tender, adding a little water to cover if necessary. This will take about an hour. Remove the vanilla pod. Process or rub the chestnuts and their juice with the honey until they are smooth. When this mixture is cool spread it over the pastry and put the pears on top, flat side down. Melt the jelly. If shop-bought jelly is used, a little water should be added. Brush this over the pears and allow to cool. Serve with thick Jersey cream.

Apple Pudding

Serves 6

This recipe comes from Anne Ward's cookery book. It is simple to make and can be eaten hot or cold with cream or good custard.

6 large cooking apples
3 oz (75 g) light brown sugar
4 oz (100 g) butter
3 eggs

Core, peel and chop the apples. Put them in a saucepan with a little water and simmer until tender. Add the butter and the sugar to taste. Stir the mixture until it is a smooth pulp and quite cool. When it is cold beat in the 3 eggs. (It must be quite cold before the eggs go in, otherwise it will curdle). Pour the mixture into a soufflé dish and sprinkle with brown sugar. Bake in a moderate oven, 350°, Gas Mark 4, for about 30 minutes, until the top looks crisp and cooked.

Wild Plum Ice Cream

Serves 6

This recipe comes from Helen Powers at Effy's Restaurant. It tastes especially good if the plums are home-picked; then you feel you have earned such a rich and delicious pudding.

1 lb (450 g) small damsons or wild plums from the hedgerow
12 oz (350 g) caster sugar
3 eggs separated
3/4 pint (450 ml) whipping cream

Put the whole fruit into a saucepan and add a small amount of water and half the sugar. Cook slowly until the fruit is soft and pulpy. Beat together the remaining sugar and egg yolks until they are thick and a pale yellow. Add this to the sieved fruit. Beat the cream but do not let it become stiff. Add cream to the fruit mixture. Beat the egg whites until stiff and fold carefully into the fruit mixture. Pour the mixture immediately into a plastic container, and freeze quickly.

Golden Valley Bananas

Serves 4

This mixture of cider and bananas is very easily made in advance.

½ pint (300 ml) sweet cider
juice of half a lemon
1 oz (25 g) granulated sugar
4 bananas
¼ pint (150 ml) whipping cream
toasted almonds

Put the cider, lemon juice, and sugar in a shallow pan and boil for five minutes. Peel and halve the bananas lengthwise. Put them into the reduced cider. Cover and simmer for three minutes. Put into a serving dish with the juice and allow to cool. Decorate with whipped cream and almonds.

Cider Apple Sorbet

Serves 6

This refreshing and unusual pudding comes from The Museum of Cider.

1½ lb (700 g) apples, peeled, cored and sliced
6 oz (175 g) granulated sugar
1 tablespoon (1 x 15 ml spoon) lemon juice
½ oz (15 g) gelatine
3 tablespoons (3 x 15 ml spoons) cold water
½ pint (300 ml) sweet cider

Put the prepared apples in a pan with the sugar and lemon juice. Cover and cook slowly until soft. Sieve or beat to a smooth purée. Leave to cool. Mix together the gelatine, apple purée, and cider, then turn into a rigid container and leave in the freezer until almost set. Turn into a large bowl and whisk until light and fluffy. Return to the container and freeze until solid. Remove from the freezer and leave to stand at room temperature for ten minutes before serving.

Rhubarb and Cider Sponge Pudding

Serves 6

This pudding comes from Susie Dunkerton and can be eaten hot or cold. The mixture of orange and rhubarb is delicious.

1½ lbs (700 g) rhubarb cut into 1" pieces
8 oz (225 g) white sugar
¼ pint (150 ml) sweet cider
3 tablespoons (3 x 15 ml spoons) orange juice
grated rind of one orange
juice of one orange

For the topping:

3 oz (75 g) butter
2 oz (50 g) brown sugar
3 eggs
4 oz (100 g) fine wholemeal flour
3 level teaspoons (3 x 5 ml spoons) baking powder
1 - 2 teaspoons (1 - 2 x 5 ml spoons) ground ginger

Put the rhubarb in a baking tin and sprinkle with the sugar. Add the orange juice, cider and rind. In a separate bowl cream the butter and sugar. Add the eggs alternately with spoonfuls of the flour and baking powder. Stir in the ginger. Add a little milk if necessary to keep the mixture soft. Spread this over the rhubarb and bake for 45 minutes at 350°, Gas Mark 4, until the sponge is golden brown.

Spinach Tansy

Serves 6

Tansy is a hardy strong-smelling herb with a distinctive taste. It was traditionally included in cakes and puddings at Eastertime in memory of the "bitter herbs" at Passover, and to help purify the system after a stodgy winter diet. The word has also come to mean a pudding or sweet omelette which is often coloured and flavoured with its juices. This one has been adapted by Patricia Hegarty from Elizabeth Foley's cookery book. It is a pretty pudding, being pale green and orange with a lightly astringent taste.

3 - 4 tablespoons (3 - 4 x 15 ml spoons) spinach juice
2 teaspoons (2 x 5 ml spoons) tansy juice
4 eggs and 3 whites
1/4 pint (150 ml) single cream
1/4 pint (150 ml) milk
sugar to taste - about 1 tablespoon (1 x 15 ml spoon)
nutmeg
1/4 pint (150 ml) fresh orange juice

Cook about ½ lb (225 g) spinach lightly and squeeze out the juice. Wet about 12 tansy leaves and squeeze out the juice. Beat together the eggs, cream, milk, sugar, nutmeg and the two green juices. Oil six moulds or custard cups and fill with the mixture. Bake in a pan half-filled with water in a oven preheated to 300°, Gas Mark 2 - 3, for thirty minutes or until set. When cool, turn out and serve with the orange juice as a sauce around each one.

Apple and Blackberry Mousse Tart

Serves 10

This tart comes from Elly Parker. A rich purple blackberry mousse takes the place of a crême patissière. It is decorated with thin slices of apple and whole blackberries and covered with an apricot glaze. It looks wonderful and tastes even better.

Pate Sucrée Base:
8 oz (225 g) plain flour
6 oz (175 g) chilled butter
2 egg yolks
2 drops vanilla essence
2 oz (50 g) caster sugar
white of an egg
pinch of salt

For the glaze:
2 tablespoons (2 x 15 ml spoons) apricot jam
1 tablespoon (1 x 15 ml spoon) sugar

For the mousse filling:
4 large dessert apples
8 oz (225 g) blackberries
caster sugar to taste
2 medium eggs separated
5 fl. oz (150 ml) double cream whipped

To make the pastry base, sift the flour and salt into a mixing bowl. Add small pieces of butter. Mix together thoroughly, or put in a food processor and blend for 10 seconds. Add the yolks, sugar, and vanilla essence. Beat together or process for 20 seconds. Chill and roll out. Put into a greased flan dish. Bake blind for 10 minutes at 400°, Gas Mark 6. Remove from oven, paint the base with egg white and bake for a further 10 minutes at 375°, Gas Mark 5. Allow to cool.

Core and peel two apples and mill half the blackberries. Cook with sugar to taste. Purée and cool.

Cream the egg yolks and two level tablespoons (2 x 15 ml spoon) of sugar until the mixture turns pale. Add the fruit. Fold in the whipped cream. In a separate bowl whip the egg whites until stiff with 1 heaped tablespoon (1 x 15 ml spoon) of sugar. Fold this into the fruit mixture and spread over the pastry base. Chill.

Core and quarter the remaining apples and slice them very thinly. Hull the blackberries. Arrange the fruit in rings on top of the mousse. Melt the jam and sugar slowly until liquid. Brush this over the fruit. Serve chilled.

Grapefruit and Mint Sorbet

Serves 8

This just the sort of dish that might have been served during a large Edwardian dinner party to refresh the palate and encourage the appetite. It is the invention of Jenny Allday, who runs Country Cooks. The combination of mint and grapefruit is delicious.

1/2 pint (300 ml) water
6 oz (175 g) granulated sugar
a good handful of mint leaves stripped from the stalk
pared rind and juice of 1 lemon
1 1/2 tubs (9 fl oz 180 ml) frozen concentrated grapefruit juice
1 egg white

Put the pared lemon rind in a saucepan with the sugar and water. Bring to the boil, stirring to dissolve the sugar. Boil for five minutes then plunge in the mint leaves. Remove from the heat. Cover and leave to infuse for twenty minutes. Strain the syrup onto the lemon and grapefruit juices. Chill, then freeze to a mush. Remove from the freezer and beat until smooth in a chilled bowl. Quickly fold in the stiffly whisked egg white. Return to the freezer to harden.

Apple and Honey Parfait

Serves 6

There are many different kinds of honey made and sold in Herefordshire. This parfait calls for a mild honey which complements the taste of the apple in a much more delicate way than ordinary sugar. It comes from Jenny Allday, who also suggests adding a little cinnamon or cloves to the apples as they stew.

1 1/2 lbs (700 g) cooking apples
a good strip of lemon rind

8 oz (225 g) mild warmed honey
4 egg yolks
1/4 pint (150 ml) water
3/4 pint (450 ml) whipping cream

Peel, core and chop the apples and stew with half the honey and the strip of lemon in just enough water to cover the bottom of the pan. When they are cooked remove the lemon rind and mash the apples to a pulp. Beat the pulp until cool. Beat the egg yolks and the remaining half of the honey till thick and creamy. Fold in the apple pulp when it is cold. Lastly, fold in the stiffly whipped cream. Chill and freeze. When the mixture is beginning to set, remove it from the freezer, beat again, then return to the freezer and leave to harden.

Apple Tansy

Serves 4

This recipe came originally from Elizabeth Foley's cookery book. Patricia Hegarty has adapted it to suit modern tastes. It needs plenty of spices, and the apple rings make it a very decorative pudding.

4 good sized dessert apples
4 eggs
1 1/2 oz (40 g) butter
a good pinch of cinnamon
grated nutmeg

Peel, core and slice the apples into rings. Fry the rings in 1 oz (25 g) butter until they are soft, but still retain their shape. Leave them in their pan on one side. Beat the eggs with the sugar and spices. Add the remaining butter to the apple rings and return to the pan to heat. When the butter is foaming, add the egg mixture. Move the rings about in the eggs at first. When the omelette is just firm, turn it over for a moment so that the apple rings can brown. Serve warm with thick cream.

Apple Cider Flan

This decorative and delicious flan calls for real artistry.

4 small tart eating apples
2 tablespoons (2 x 15 ml spoons) sugar
1/2 pint (300 ml) cider
1/2 pint (300 ml) thick cold custard, preferably homemade
6 glacé cherries
1/4 pint (150 ml) whipped cream
apricot jam
angelica
9" baked pastry case

Peel, core and halve the apples. Combine the sugar and cider and bring to the boil. Poach the apples very gently in the cider syrup for 8 - 10 minutes, or until they are tender but not soft. Remove carefully and set aside. Brush the inside of the baked pastry case with warm apricot jam. Cover with the custard and arrange the cooked apple halves flat side down on top. Allow to settle. Place a cherry between each apple and decorate with piped whipped cream and angelica. Reduce the cider syrup to a thick glaze and pour a little over each apple. Chill slightly before serving.

Cakes

Brampton Bryan Cherry Cake

In the Hereford Records Office I was given a box of papers taken from Brampton Bryan Post Office when it was sold in 1964. Miss Edwards had lived there since the death of her father in the 1920s. He had been the postman, shoemaker and shopkeeper for the village. When the house was opened up after his daughter's death, it was discovered that everything was exactly as it had been in the 1920s. In the forty years since her father's death Miss Edwards had changed nothing and kept everything.

I discovered this recipe, handwritten in a child's exercise book, by literally blowing the dust off the cover to see what was underneath.

The cherry cake uses half plain flour and half ground rice. It is very moist with a distinctive flavour and extremely popular with children.

8 oz (225 g) plain flour sifted
8 oz (225 g) ground rice
8 oz (225 g) butter
4 eggs
1 teaspoon (1 x 5 ml spoon) baking powder
few drops vanilla essence
a dozen glacé cherries cut into quarters

Grease a 9" cake tin and line the bottom with a circle of greaseproof paper. Cream the butter and sugar together until pale and creamy. Add the eggs one by one and beat well. Put in the ground rice and beat for fifteen minutes. The mixture will become quite runny. Finally add the flour, baking powder and vanilla essence, and lightly stir in the cherries. Bake in a preheated oven, 325°, Gas Mark 4, for 1½ hours. If the top begins to brown, cover the cake with a piece of foil. Allow to cool in the tin for 20 minutes before inverting it onto a wire rack. This cake will keep for 3 or 4 days if it is well wrapped.

Cider Cake

This versatile recipe for a cider cake comes from Ros Fry. It can also be turned into a pudding by baking in a 1½ pint (900 ml) ring mould and filling the centre with puréed apples mixed with cream or yoghurt and decorated with flaked almonds. This is not the sweetest of cakes, but it has a subtle flavour and is very good on a picnic with apples and cider.

¼ pint (150 ml) cider
4 oz (100 g) butter
4 oz (100 g) soft brown sugar
2 beaten eggs
8 oz (225 g) plain flour sifted
1 teaspoon (1 x 5 ml spoon) bicarbonate of soda
1 teaspoon (1 x 5 ml spoon) grated nutmeg

Cream the butter and sugar until light and creamy. Add half the flour, sifted with the soda and the nutmeg. Pour the cider over the mixture and beat thoroughly until the acid of the cider acts on the alkali of the soda and makes the mixture frothy. Stir in the remaining flour and quickly pour the mixture into a well-greased baking tin. Bake in a preheated oven 350°, Gas Mark 5, for 45 minutes or until cooked. When the cake is ready it should shrink slightly from the sides of the tin. Allow to cool in the tin for five minutes and turn out onto a wire rack.

Honey Fruit Cake

Herefordshire is very proud of its beekeeping tradition and is lucky enough to have many of its hedgerows intact, so there is still excellent foraging for bees in search of nectar. The Herefordshire Honey Show is held in October at the College for the Blind in Hereford. This is the recipe given for the Honey Fruit Cake competition, which is part of the Show every year.

8 oz (225 g) self-raising flour
5 oz (125 g) butter or margarine
2 eggs
8 oz (225 g) honey
4 oz (100 g) sultanas
4 oz (100 g) currants
2 oz (50 g) peel
pinch of nutmeg
pinch of salt
milk if necessary

Grease a 7" round baking tin. Cream the butter and the honey. Beat in the eggs and the sifted flour, salt and nutmeg, alternating with the fruit and peel. Mix well, adding milk if necessary. Bake in a moderate oven, 325°, Gas Mark 3, for about two hours.

Hereford Curd Cakes

The recipe for these traditional curd cakes comes from Ann Searle at the Agricultural College at Holme Lacy. They are also a very good way of using up milk that has gone sour.

For the shortcrust pastry:

5 oz (125 g) plain flour
2 oz (50 g) butter or margarine
pinch of salt
cold water to mix

Curd filling:

2 pints (1.2 litres) sour milk
1 egg
1 tablespoon (1 x 15 ml spoon) brandy or rum
1 dessertspoon (1 x 10 ml spoon) grated lemon rind
2 oz (50 g) butter
1 tablespoon (1 x 15 ml spoon) currants
1 oz (25 g) caster sugar
pinch of salt
pinch of nutmeg
1 tablespoon (1 x 15 ml spoon) milk

Place the sour milk in a piece of muslin and hang up to drain for 24 hours. Make the pastry and line two sandwich tins with it. Break up the curd and beat it in with the butter. Add the remaining ingredients including the well-beaten egg. Spoon the curd mixture into the pastry cases and put a little grated nutmeg on top of each cake. Bake in a fairly hot oven, 400°, Gas Mark 6, for ten minutes, then lower heat to 350°, Gas Mark 4 and bake for thirty minutes until the mixture is set and the pastry is cooked.

A "Seedness" Cake

Cakes and biscuits flavoured with caraway seed are a part of Herefordshire tradition. It has been suggested that the description "seedness" may also refer to the time of sowing as the cake was often eaten during rural festivities celebrating the end of sowing. In his book, *Joyce Jeffries of Ham Castle* the Rev. R. J. Griffiths gives an account of Joyce Jeffries, in the mid seventeenth century, presenting the sum of one shilling to a dairymaid called Bes Jones for "the well making of the seedness cake."

8 oz (225 g) self raising flour sifted
6 oz (150 g) caster sugar
6 oz (150 g) butter
3 eggs
2 teaspoons (2 x 5 ml spoons) caraway seeds
1 heaped tablespoon (1 x 15 ml spoon) ground almonds
2 - 3 tablespoons (2 - 3 x 15 ml spoons) milk
4 oz (100 g) candied lemon peel to decorate

Grease and line a medium sized loaf tin. Cream the butter and sugar together until it is pale and creamy. Add the eggs one by one. Then add the caraway seeds and the ground almonds, and finally the sifted flour and enough milk to keep the mixture soft. Spoon into the tin and level it off with a knife. Decorate with the lemon peel. Preheat the oven to 350°, Gas Mark 4, and bake in the centre of the oven for about one hour or until the cake springs back when lightly pressed in the middle. Allow the cake to cool in the tin before turning it onto a wire rack.

A Genuine Old Cake

This recipe comes from *The Hereford Times* of 1908 and was said then to be "from a genuine old recipe". It is a very moist cake and keeps well. Treacle can be substituted for golden syrup if a darker cake is wanted.

1 lb (450 g) plain flour sifted
4 oz (100 g) butter
8 oz (225 g) light brown sugar
4 tablespoons (4 x 15 ml spoons) golden syrup
6 eggs
1 lb (450 g) currants
2 oz (50 g) candied peel
6 glacé cherries chopped
2 oz (50 g) sweet almonds

Cream the butter and the sugar. When light and creamy, add the golden syrup. Beat in the eggs one by one. Mix in the currants, candied peel, nuts and cherries. Lastly sift the flour and mix it in, stirring as little as possible. Place the mixture in a lined and well-buttered cake tin with a removable base. Bake uncovered in a cool oven, 250 - 275°, Gas Mark 1, for almost five hours. Allow to cool slightly before removing from the tin. This cake will keep in an airtight cake tin for up to a month (if you can stop yourself eating it !)

Mrs. Winington's Gingerbread

This recipe comes from Elizabeth Foley's cookery book. The original, attributed to Mrs. Winington, calls for 2 lbs of treacle, and would have been a mighty cake. I have scaled the proportions down but the method and ingredients remain essentially the same.

10 oz (275 g) self-raising flour
8 oz (225 g) black treacle
2 oz (50 g) brown sugar
4 oz (100 g) butter
2 eggs
two good pinches each of ground cloves and ground mace
1 level teaspoon (1 x 5 ml spoon) caraway seeds
1 teaspoon (1 x 5 ml) powdered ginger
1 tablespoon (1 x 15 ml) candied peel
2 tablespoons (2 x 15 ml spoons) sultanas or raisins

Melt the butter and add to the sugar and treacle. Mix well and add the eggs one by one. Sift the ground spices with the flour and sprinkle over the treacle mixture and stir. Add the mixed peel and raisins and mix in lightly. Grease and flour a medium- sized cake tin and line the bottom with butter paper. Bake in a moderate oven, 325°, Gas Mark 3, for 1½ hours. Allow to cool before removing from the tin.

Neffy's Brandy Truffles

On most days in Effy's Restaurant in Hereford you will find a lovely Australian called Neffy concocting exotic drinks behind the bar. She also makes some of the best brandy truffles in the Northern Hemisphere.

6½ oz (185 g) dark chocolate
2 oz (50 g) butter
3 tablespoons (3 x 15 ml spoons) cream
3 tablespoons (3 x 15 ml spoons) icing sugar
1 tablespoon (1 x 15 ml spoons) brandy
cocoa powder

Melt the chocolate and butter in a double saucepan. Add the cream. When the mixture is cool, mix in the icing sugar carefully. Finally add the brandy. Leave in a cool place overnight. Roll the mixture into small balls and dredge in the cocoa powder. Serve with coffee after dinner. (These quantities make approximately two dozen truffles.)

Sponge Biscuits

Mrs. Iris Jones, of Garnons, told me that in the days before the whisk, cooks used to beat their sponge mixtures with a practised flick of the wrist, drawing their fingers through the mixture many times until it was light and fluffy. Sometimes this process would take half an hour or more. The technique was a closely guarded secret which many cooks refused to pass on to their assistants - who were literally aching to find it out.

4 oz (100 g) plain flour, sifted
5 oz (125 g) icing sugar, sifted
3 eggs separated
3 drops vanilla

Sift the flour and half the sugar together three times. Beat the egg whites until stiff, gradually adding the remaining sugar. Beat the egg yolks until thick and creamy and add the vanilla. Lightly fold this mixture into the egg whites. Sift the flour, a third at a time, over the eggs and fold in carefully. Spoon into shapes on a baking tray and bake at 350°, Gas Mark 5, for 12 - 15 minutes. Allow the biscuits to cool on a rack.

Chocolate Wafers

When a friend tasted these biscuits, he said they reminded him of the kind his grandmother used to make. The recipe comes from *The Hereford Times* in 1906 - about the time my friend's grandmother might have been learning the art of baking. The recipe calls for grated chocolate and the wafers are rich, light and crisp. It makes about 24 wafers.

3 oz (75 g) caster sugar
3 oz (75 g) brown sugar
3 oz (75 g) butter
3 oz (75 g) grated dark chocolate
1 egg
1 teaspoon (1 x 5 ml spoon) vanilla
4½ oz (115 g) plain flour

Refrigerate the bar of chocolate so that it is easier to grate. Cream the butter and sugar together. Add the egg, then the vanilla, the flour and finally the chocolate. Lift the dough with floured hands and roll out thinly (handle it as little as possible, to stop the chocolate melting). Cut into squares or use biscuit cutters. Place on a greased baking tray and bake in a moderate oven, 350°, Gas Mark 5, for 10 minutes. Remove the biscuits onto a rack to cool.

Drinks, Pickles and Preserves

Sack Posset

This recipe is adapted from Elizabeth Foley's. The original calls for the addition of "oringoe roots slic'd very thin." These were the candied roots of the sea-holly, which can easily be found on sandy beaches, as any bare-footed bather will confirm. In the early sixteenth century it was very popular as an aphrodisiac, so much so that a local candying industry grew up in Colchester which lasted into the middle of the nineteenth century. The quantities given below are for one person.

1 egg separated
1 tablespoon (1 x 15 ml spoon) caster sugar
1/4 pint (150 ml) milk
2 tablespoons (2 x 15 ml spoons) sherry
nutmeg

In a small bowl beat the yolk until light. Gradually add the sugar, sherry, and milk. Whip the egg white until stiff and fold lightly into the other ingredients. Pour into a glass and sprinkle a few grains of nutmeg on top.

Hot Cider Punch

This delicious recipe for mulled cider comes from Ivor Dunkerton.

4 pints (2.2 litres) dry cider
1/2 pint (300 ml) light rum
1 dessertspoon (1 x 10 ml spoon) orange bitters
or 1/4 pint (150 ml) orange juice
2 tablespoons (2 x 15 ml spoons) honey to taste
4 whole allspice
6 cloves
2 cinnamon sticks

Put the cider, rum. orange bitters or orange juice, allspice, cloves, honey and half of one cinnamon stick in a large pan and heat thoroughly but do not allow to boil. Warm a large serving bowl and break in the remaining cinnamon sticks. Pour in the hot cider and serve immediately.

Sangria

This popular party drink comes from the Museum of Cider.

2 lemons, sliced
2 oranges, sliced
2 apples, cored and sliced
12 ice cubes
4 pints (2 litres) sweet cider
2 bottles cheap red wine
1 glass brandy
2 - 4 tablespoons (2 - 4 x 15 ml spoons) caster sugar

Chill the cider and wine well. Place all ingredients together in a very large mixing bowl and stir thoroughly. Serve at once in wine glasses.

Pickled Mushrooms

This recipe comes from Anne Ward's cookery book. Pickled mushrooms go splendidly with pâtés and cold meats, or can be eaten on their own with bread and butter. While this recipe calls for field mushrooms, commercially grown mushrooms may be used instead.

4 lbs (1.75 kilos) field mushrooms
1 heaped tablespoon (1 x 15 ml spoon) salt
2 medium onions thinly sliced
1¾ pints (1 litre) red wine vinegar
1 tablespoon (1 x 15 ml spoon) cayenne pepper
6 whole allspice

Clean the mushrooms and make sure they are dry. If you are using big ones, cut the ragged ends off the stems and quarter them. Put them in a large dish and sprinkle them liberally with salt. Set aside for at least six hours. Strain the liquid from the mushrooms and reduce to half over a medium heat. Add the vinegar, onion, cayenne pepper and the allspice. Finally add the mushrooms, and stew them over a low heat for ten minutes. Lift out the mushrooms and onions and pack them into hot, sterilized jars. Return the liquid to the heat and bring to the boil. Fill the jars to the top, pressing down the contents to release any air bubbles. Seal and leave for at least two weeks before using. This is a marvellous way of preserving mushrooms when they are plentiful.

Pickled Crab Apples

Crab apples are the common wild apples of Northern Europe and the ancestors of all dessert and cooking apples. They are inedible, being extremely tart and astringent, and take their name from those members of the human race who are also on the sour side. Pickled apples are easily made, and especially good with cold pork.

3 lbs (1.5 kilos) crab apples
1 lb (450 g) sugar
1 lemon wedge
1 piece bruised root ginger
1 cinnamon stick
2 cloves
4 whole allspice
1 pint (600 ml) cider vinegar

Choose small, unbruised apples. Wipe clean and place in a saucepan with the sugar and vinegar. Put the spices and lemon in a small muslin bag and add to the vinegar. Bring to the boil and simmer until the apples are just tender. Leave overnight. Remove the apples with a slotted spoon and place them in jars. A piece of ginger may be added to each jar at this point. Strain the cooking liquid, and boil down to a syrup consistency. Cover the fruit with the syrup and seal immediately. Store in a cool place for six weeks before using.

Pickled Walnuts

Four hundred years ago it was believed that a walnut, eaten whole after a large meal, would close the stomach and aid digestion. While Anne Ward would certainly not have held with such a notion, she certainly liked pickled walnuts, as there are a number of recipes for them in her book. Walnuts, preserved in this way, are an excellent addition to a plain beef stew, giving it a distinctive and unusual flavour. Pick green walnuts from the middle of June to mid- July, before the shell hardens, and remember to wear rubber gloves as walnut stain is virtually indelible.

2 lbs (almost 1 kilo) green walnuts
1 pint (600 ml) red wine or cider vinegar
1 tablespoon (1 x 15 ml spoon) pickling spice
brine made from 3 oz (75 g) salt to 1 pint (600 ml) water

Prick the walnuts all over with a large needle. Throw away any nut that has a hard end where the shell begins to develop. Soak in the brine for three days. Drain and cover with fresh brine for a further six days. Drain again, and spread the walnuts out on a cloth to expose them to the air so they turn black.

Gently boil the vinegar with the pickling spice for five minutes. Strain and allow to cool. Pack the nuts into jars, fill up to the top with the spiced vinegar, and seal at once. Allow two months before eating.

Mushroom Ketchup

This recipe comes from Anne Ward's cookery book. "Ketchup" was originally a brine of pickled fish from China which was introduced to England in the early eighteenth century. Later, ketchup came to mean any brine or vinegar-based sauce that would keep a long time and could be used as a general purpose seasoning. Commercial brands appeared in the late eighteenth and early nineteenth century, and it soon became a vital ingredient in the endless round of meals on the long voyages to and from India at the height of the British Raj.

Mushroom ketchup can be used in strong stews and soups, and is also a very good way of making use of field mushrooms when they are plentiful.

3 lbs (1.5 kilos) field mushrooms
4 oz (125 g) salt
1 tablespoon (1 x 15 ml spoon) pickling spice
1 blade mace
level teaspoon (1x 5 ml spoon) ginger
1/2 pint (300 ml) vinegar
1/2 pint (300 ml) rough red wine
1 onion, chopped

Trim and wipe the mushrooms. Roughly chop and sprinkle liberally with salt. Leave in a large pot for two days, stirring occasionally. Gently boil the vinegar with the pickling spice, mace, ginger and chopped onion. Leave for one day to infuse. Strain. Mash the mushrooms with a wooden spoon. Add the vinegar and red wine and cook for about two hours until it is thick but still runny. Sieve and pour into hot bottles, filling them not quite to the top. Seal and sterilize by placing the bottles on a folded cloth in a saucepan with enough hot water to come to within an inch of their tops. Boil very gently for twenty minutes. Leave for six weeks before using.

Effy's Spicy Marinade

Effy's have made a speciality of their marinades and mustards. A good marinade makes a world of difference to the taste and texture of meat when it is cooked. This particular one can be used for chicken or lamb before making into kebabs or barbecuing. It is also a way of preserving meat for up to seven days in the fridge.

1/4 pint (150 ml) vegetable oil
1/2 pint (300 ml) plain yoghurt
1 tablespoon (1 x 15 ml spoon) dried or grained mustard
1 1/2 tablespoons (1.5 x 15 ml spoons) fresh ginger finely chopped
level dessertspoon (1 x 10 ml spoon) cumin
level dessertspoon (1 x 10 ml spoon) ground turmeric
level dessertspoon (1 x 10 ml spoon) freshly ground coriander
1 green chilli seeded and chopped
juice of one lemon
salt and pepper

Pound together the spices and the mustard and add the oil followed by the lemon juice. Finally add the yoghurt. Alternatively, put all the spices and mustard and oil into a blender. While blending add the lemon juice. Pour this liquid into the yoghurt. Be sure each piece of meat is thoroughly covered with the marinade. If it is gently reheated and not allowed to boil, the marinade can be used as a sauce for the meat.

Effy's Mustard

This delicious mustard calls for some unusual ingredients which may well have to be ordered in advance from the nearest wholefood store.

1½ oz (40 g) pickling spice
4½ oz (115 g) black mustard seed
4½ oz (115 g) white mustard seed
1½ oz (40 g) sea salt
3 oz (75 g) Molasses
1 pint (600 ml) cider vinegar

Put all the ingredients into a china bowl or large jar and leave in a cool place for at least a week. Blend the ingredients in a blender or magimix until the mixture is still grainy but the mustard seeds have been cracked.

Store in jars with tight lids. Do not leave metal spoons in the mustard, or serve in a metal dish.

Index

Beef:
- Brisket with Orange, 49
- Effyburgers, 51
- Herefordshire Beef Olives, 50

Cabbage:
- Red, Anne Ward's, 53

Cakes, Breads & Biscuits:
- Brampton Bryan Cherry Cake, 73
- Chocolate Wafers, 82
- Cider Cake, 74
- Genuine Old Cake, 78
- Hereford Curd Cakes, 76
- Honey Fruit Cake, 75
- Mrs. Winington's Gingerbread, 79
- "Seedness" Cake, 77
- Sponge Biscuits, 81

Chicken:
- Chicken Breasts with Calvados, 33
- Chicken Pie, 37
- Chicken with Prunes, 34
- Country Cooks' Chicken, 34
- Elizabeth Foley's Stuffed Chicken, 35

Drinks:
- Hot Cider Punch, 84
- Sack Posset, 83
- Sangria, 85

Fish:
- Cod or Pike Baked in Spinach, 23
- Eel, grilled, 29
- Eel, smoked, 28
- Grayling, à la Meunière, 26
- Grayling, grilled, 26
- Herrings, pickled, 27
- Herring Roes with Lemon, 22
- Jenny Allday's Fish Pie, 30
- Mackerel with Gooseberry Sauce, 25
- Pike, cold with Mayonnaise, 29
- Trout, pickled, 24
- Trout, potted, 21

Ice Cream:
- Ginger, 58
- Wild Plum, 65

Lamb:
- Collared Breast of Lamb with Onion Sauce, 47
- Harigo Lamb, 45
- Lamb with Port, 43
- Lamb Noisettes in Perry Sauce, 44
- Lamb Steaks in Puff Pastry, 46

Pasta:
- Broad Beans with Pasta, 55
- Walnut Sauce with Pasta, 56

Patés, Terrines and Potted Meat:
- Hare Paté, 19
- Pheasant Terrine, 18
- Potted Tongue and Chicken, Calamanco, 17

Pies, Flans and Tarts:
- Apple and Blackberry Mousse Tart, 68
- Apple Cider Flan, 72
- Chicken Pie, 37
- Hope End Pear and Chestnut Flan, 63
- Leominster Custard Pie, 60
- Raspberry and Redcurrant Pie, 58

Pigeon:
- Pigeon Casserole, 38
- Pigeon with Lovage in Perry Sauce, 39

Pork:
- Roast Pork with Thyme, 48

Preserves:
- Effy's Mustard, 91
- Effy's Spicy Marinade, 90
- Mushroom Ketchup, 89
- Pickled Crab Apples, 87
- Pickled Mushrooms, 86
- Pickled Walnuts, 88

Rabbit:
- Cider Rabbit Stew, 40

Soufflés:
- Spinach and Sorrel Soufflé, 54

Soups:
- Almond Soup, 16
- Cod and Mussel Soup, 13
- Elizabeth Foley's Pea Soup, 15
- Gatley Park Turnip Soup, 14
- Sorrel Soup, 12
- Uncle Dick's Onion Soup, 12

Starters:
- Cider Garlic Bread, 11
- Potted Mushrooms, 17
- Ros Fry's Winter Salad, 20

Sweets & Puddings:
- Apple and Honey Parfait, 70
- Apple Pudding, 64
- Apple Tansy, 71
- Cider Apple Sorbet, 66
- Ginger Pear Upside Down Pudding, 61
- Golden Valley Bananas, 66
- Grapefruit and Mint Sorbet, 70
- Neffy's Brandy Truffles, 80
- Orange and Lemon Cream, 62
- Orange Pudding, 59
- Rhubarb and Cider Sponge, 69
- Spinach Tansy, 68

Venison:
- Venison Pasty, 41